Living Loving & Ageing

Sexual and Personal Relationships in Later Life

Wendy Greengross and Sally Greengross

To Ira with love

Sally

x x x x

AGE Concern

© 1989 Wendy Greengross and Sally Greengross

Published by Age Concern England
Bernard Sunley House
60 Pitcairn Road
Mitcham, Surrey CR4 3LL

Design Eugenie Dodd
Editorial assistance Dorothy Baldock
Production Joyce O'Shaughnessy
Illustrations Mary-Lou North
Cover photography Geoff Franklin
Word processing Christine Blane
Typeset from disc by Phil Richards, London SW16
Printed by Ebenezer Baylis & Son Ltd, Worcester

ISBN 086242-070-9

'One of the compensations of growing old is that ...
the passions remain as strong as ever, but one has
gained – at last – the power which adds a supreme
flavour to existence – the power of taking hold of
experience and of turning it round, slowly, in the
light.'

Virginia Woolf

About the Authors

Wendy Greengross qualified as a doctor in 1949 and worked as a GP for over 35 years. She trained as a counsellor and was a regular panel member of Radio 4's "If You Think You've Got Problems" throughout the 1970s. She was also "Dr Wendy" of *The Sun*. She is a Trustee of the Leonard Cheshire Foundation and has worked with many organisations concerned with disability.

Wendy Greengross's book, *Entitled to Love*, published in 1976, dealt with the sexual and emotional problems of disabled people and was instrumental in helping to change attitudes to disability. She was founder chairman of SPOD (Association to Aid the Sexual and Personal Relationships of People with a Disability) and has written extensively on counselling, sexuality, parenting, marriage and disability.

She has been involved in teaching pastoral care and counselling for nearly 20 years and was a member of the Warnock Committee which reported on social, legal and ethical implications of human fertilisation and embryology. She was widowed in 1982 after 31 years of marriage and has five children and two grandchildren.

Sally Greengross joined Age Concern England 12 years ago and became Director in 1987. Her earlier background included lecturing, research and work with children, families and young offenders. She is Joint Chairman of the Board of the Age Concern Institute of Gerontology, King's College London, a member of the Standing Advisory Committee on Transport for Disabled and Elderly People and a Fellow of the Royal Society of Health.

She is General Secretary of "Eurolink-Age" a European Community-wide organisation working with politicians, administrators and older people's organisations at a European level and International Vice President of the International Federation on Ageing with responsibility for its European office. The IFA is a world-wide non-governmental organisation recognised by the main UN bodies and agencies, including the World Health Organisation which she frequently represents at an International and National level.

Author of numerous books and articles, she writes, lectures and broadcasts frequently, both here and in other countries, on a wide range of issues concerning policy and practice relating to older people.

Sally Greengross is married with four children.

C<u>ontents</u>

Preface

There are many books and magazine articles which give guidance on sexuality and personal relationships, but they tend to be aimed at younger readers. This book is written for older people who want to know more about sexuality and their own capacity to enjoy this aspect of their lives. It is also for the younger generation who are looking forward to their own ageing and want to achieve their full potential for joyous relationships in later life.

It examines emotional and psychological tensions and physical problems which may arise, but it is not a book about disability and problems alone, rather about ordinary people and their need for affection and intimacy as they grow older.

Carers may also find it helpful when faced with difficult dilemmas posed by close proximity to elderly people with explicit sexual and emotional needs. They may be uncertain whether they should be supportive and encouraging in their approach, or whether they should discourage something that is difficult to accept and sometimes to understand.

In this book we take no particular standpoint, but draw attention to needs which some people experience and pinpoint various choices which are open to them. We also identify some available options and highlight possible ways of achieving a happier life through the exploration of relationships and friendships.

We have attempted to look at a whole range of problems and difficulties. These will be thought about and interpreted differently depending on the way people have previously approached their own sexuality and that of others. Attitudes will also be affected by differing religious and cultural beliefs. It is not our intention to criticise any such views.

It is highly unlikely that everything discussed in this book will be accepted by everyone who reads it, as sexuality and the forming of relationships are individual and personal.

Many people will not be used to the frank and explicit way in which issues about sexuality are approached. This is in no way intended to cause offence and we hope that people will use this book in the way they find most helpful, taking from it only what is valuable to them. No-one can ever be certain about what another person wants and desires.

Although this book is primarily for the older reader and for those who work with and care for older people, there is a strong message in it for everyone. Older adults are no different from younger adults in having the right to choose their own lifestyle and set their own standards.

Wendy Greengross and Sally Greengross

'You take your's off first!'

1. Scene Setting

'To see a young couple loving each other is no wonder, but to see an old couple loving each other is the best sight of all.'

William Makepeace Thackeray

*T*here are times in our lives when we need to take stock of ourselves, of who we are and where we are going; to think about what we value most, what needs to be cherished and what can be discarded. This applies to all aspects of living, but particularly to personal relationships.

As we age there will probably be fewer people we care about deeply than there were when we were young, but they become increasingly precious to us. Their importance may be rooted in a long family life history shared with a sister or brother; it may lie in a friendship which began many years ago.

Those of us who are parents will by now have learned to accept our children as adults of equal status, and know that expressions of love, support and care between the generations have to adapt to change over the years. This love within the family is for many of us the source of our greatest joy as we grow old. If it is solidly based, it will easily withstand the shift which takes place as the balance in family caring and support swings, usually imperceptibly at first, like a slow-moving see-saw, from the older to the younger members of the family.

Loving relationships

Those of us fortunate in having long lasting and successful marriages will have outgrown the need to impress or try to change the other, having by now learnt tolerance of areas where we differ. A distinct advantage as we get older is to have someone with whom we can be totally honest. This can help us in accepting ourselves more easily as the people we are, rather than those we used to have hopes of becoming.

A close relationship with our partner is for many of us the foundation stone on which we build the last part of our lives. Among those who have lost their partners, there are many who, understandably, feel deprived of an essential aspect of life, the emotional and spiritual bedrock of love and tenderness between two people.

Sexuality

Our sexuality is an important aspect of that closeness and can be the key to how we transmit the affection we feel to the person we love.

The ability to do this does not disappear either with age or as circumstances change, but the way we think about it can affect our capacity to accept it positively either in ourselves or in others.

Even as a topic of discussion, sexuality is likely to arouse strong emotions. As we reach later life, some of us may believe that our physical sex life is over. Others know that this need not be true, and continue to enjoy happy and fulfilling sexual relationships, but many of us are trapped because we cannot consider sexuality positively and are unable to explore the wide range of possibilities that could be available. We feel inhibited by the whole subject and are afraid of anything new or different. We may need reassurance that it is normal to look at these aspects of our personality and our needs in order to decide whether or not we wish to make changes in our lifestyle.

Changes in attitudes

We are all affected by the values and attitudes we absorbed from our parents, many of which they in turn learned from their parents. Today's older generation will, therefore, have been influenced by views which were widely held at the end of the last century. They have also been subjected to more mixed messages about values and appropriate behaviour, more buffeting about sexuality and sexual responses, than any previous generation. Many of us were brought up when masturbation was considered a sin and sex before marriage, particularly for women, looked upon as morally reprehensible.

Gradually the increasingly widespread use of contraceptives began to affect the way people thought about sexuality, and made it possible to separate sex from child-bearing. Then suddenly the confusing 'enlightenment' of the fifties and sixties appeared to make everything and anything acceptable. We were all confronted with changing values and people began to accept that sexuality was something to be enjoyed as a physical pleasure for women as well as for men.

The latest swing of the pendulum has been brought about through anxiety about AIDS, and the fear that sexuality may be dangerous. Many people are now wondering whether sex is something to be enjoyed or whether it is something to be afraid of and avoided.

Images of beauty

It is easy to get the impression from TV, films and advertising that sex is only for the young and beautiful. We do not see boxes of chocolates or exotic drinks being given to disabled people or to those who are old or ugly.

Society sets standards and it is unfortunate for all those who do not conform that beauty is identified very often nowadays with being young and slim, lithe and unwrinkled. This is as constricting for young people as for the old, but the truth is that as we age we do tend to become less attractive in the conventionally accepted way. Because we sag in places where we used to be firm, getting lined and wrinkled, this may create doubts in our own minds not only as to whether we are still loveable, but also whether older people should be enjoying sex and passion at all.

Negative attitudes

It is also important to recognise that negative attitudes surrounding older people and sexuality are widespread and very damaging. These are held by people of all ages, and can make it difficult to get the help or advice we need because some professionals and other advisers, along with many older people themselves, share the mistaken belief that sex stops at 60 – if not before. Any of them may find it difficult to accept that people in later life have sexual desires and drives. They may even find it rather disgusting.

Older people are encouraged to take up new interests which may be intellectually stimulating or of value to the community and which keep idle hands employed. Yet there is still a taboo on translating that into the development of personal relationships and the realms of sexual exploration.

When we are young we feel resentful when other people try to enforce their beliefs on us and tell us how we ought to lead our lives. How much worse it is, therefore, for those of us who survive into later years, to find that people seem to take over and tell us what to do.

Adapting to change

There are some changes that we are forced to make, as we get older – to adapt to retirement, the loss of a partner or the move to a new environment. There are also times when personal relationships need to change in order to cope with new situations.

The important thing is to realise that, although we are often faced with making choices between unpleasant or unwelcome alternatives, there are also positive choices we can make. The more we exercise our right to choose, the longer we will keep our independence.

Stereotypes

Stereotyped images of older people can be very damaging. While people of the same generation have much in common in terms of shared history, it should not be forgotten that they also have widely different cultural backgrounds, and in some cases come from different countries of origin. Neither gender nor race nor colour are reliable clues as to how people feel about sexuality. Their upbringing will differ. The colour of their skin and their white hair will say no more about their attitudes and feelings than does the colour of their eyes, but cross-cultural expectations can be very misleading. Sadly, many older people from ethnic minorities suffer not only racism but also ageism, which is a virulent and very widespread form of discrimination against those who are old.

One of the prime aims of this book is to give people the confidence they need to combat these negative attitudes and expectations, when directed at older people, whatever their colour, creed or sexual orientation. Everyone needs to be regarded as an individual regardless of his or her age.

Surprise that the face in the mirror seems so old.

2. <u>*Ageing*</u>

'No Spring, nor Summer beauty hath such
grace,
As I have seen in one autumnal face.'

John Donne

*M*ore people than ever before now survive into old age. This is a major triumph of the twentieth century, a worldwide revolution which was not brought about by war but by peaceful measures such as medical advances, including the introduction of antibiotics, social security benefits and the widespread development of health and social care programmes. In the industrialised world the whole balance of the population has been reversed. In the past there were large numbers of children and very few old people. Many were deprived of growing into adulthood by sweeping infections which ravaged the whole population. Killer diseases like tuberculosis have now virtually been eradicated. Everywhere the numbers of old people relative to the young are escalating and at the same time family planning techniques have dramatically reduced the numbers of children born. Life expectation at the turn of the century was 48 for men and 51.6 for women. At that time roughly 35 per cent of the population were under 15, but the numbers of people of 60 and over have increased fourfold since then. So old people have lost the scarcity value they had in the past. In those days the skills they taught were of lasting value and of supreme importance to the next generation, who needed to acquire them in order to survive. Today the speed of change is so fast that the skills we all need become out of date more quickly than any of us could have imagined. Even young parents need to retrain if they are to keep up with the technological skills their children learn from an early age at school.

Keeping up with change

Given all this, it is not really surprising that the knowledge many older people have can be easily dismissed as obsolete, whether it is or not. What is much worse is that older people themselves are often considered to be just as out of date as their skills. They are labelled as useless and anachronistic, in much the same way as the arithmetic they learned at school has become to computer-wise teenagers. Old people are also often assumed to be rigid and unable to change their ways, which is both cruel and false, as they have lived through more change more rapidly than any previous generation. Not only have they lived through it but they have adapted to it in an extraordinarily flexible way, having in their own lives seen the development of broadcasting from steam radio to satellite TV; of travel from trains to supersonic flight. They have also witnessed the wonder of electric gadgets give way to the use of equipment designed for an electronic space age. Among today's retired people are the pioneers, skilled workers and experts who made it all happen. They have an immense 'bank' of knowledge, wisdom and experience which they could pass on to the next generation, but often lack the opportunity to do so and are forced to conform to widely held expectations, including the totally incorrect assumption that most elderly people are likely to be frail and dependent on others.

Facts about ageing

The vast majority of older people live in their own homes and are quite capable of coping alone or with very little support. Only a small minority, mostly among those who are very old, are chronically sick or suffer from serious disabilities, although these conditions may make it very difficult for them to maintain the full lifestyle that younger people take for granted. Yet even amongst those who are most frail and disadvantaged through physical or mental frailty, only a very small proportion, under 5 per cent of the entire elderly population, are in any form of long stay institutional care. Older people in our society are in fact healthier, more active and more resourceful and energetic than has ever been the case in the past. Many are just as fit as those who are still working and they have an enormous amount to offer. They are potentially the most important underused human resource in today's society.

The ageing process

For most of us the ageing process occurs gradually and we are not conscious of it happening at all. We find it difficult to believe that the year of our birth is so far away and are surprised that the face that stares back at us in the mirror seems so old or the reflection in the shop window so stooped. Most of the time we do not feel old, although some things may take much longer to do than previously. We feel the same inside. The difference is often in the way others treat us. This may be because other people have such difficulty in coming to terms with their own ageing and with their feelings about people they love growing old. By labelling others as old and useless they can imagine themselves to be young and effective.

Stereotypes and differences

The word 'old' arouses strong negative feelings, leading to stereo- types and generalisations which give a totally false impression of almost 10 million people in Britain today who are over retirement age. Their capabilities, skills and attitudes tend to be lumped together as if they were all alike. Yet those 10 million old people are as different from each other as 10 million young people aged between 0 and 30 or 10 million middle-aged people between 30 and 60. Given the enormous variation among older people in age, temperament and personality, it is extra- ordinary that when we reach a certain age we are all considered to be asexual. For people who hold this view there are no problems about sexuality in later life – it doesn't exist. This attitude is widespread, but it is far from the truth. In some parts of the world it is considered quite normal for old men to father children and for people to marry and enjoy an active sex life at a very advanced age. In Western society, however, the idea of old people engaging in any kind of sexually motivated behaviour is often found distasteful.

Sexual feelings

Many couples enjoy sex more as they get older, finding this aspect of their lives rewarding and fulfilling and as important to them as to younger couples. For although orgasm may be less frequent and less intense, the ability to relax and enjoy the pleasure of touching and caressing without the pressure to perform can bring joy and tranquillity unknown in earlier years. Of course there are some people who have never felt the need for physical intimacy. This does not mean that they are not capable of enjoying deep friendships and close emotional relationships. Many remain celibate from choice and others because they never met anyone with whom they wished to share that aspect of their lives. Such people are probably not going to feel a deep loss of physical sexual enjoyment as they age, and they are just as normal as those who do.

Life today

Nowadays families tend to live in small units and because so many people move away to seek work, large numbers of elderly people live a long way from their families and have to find new roles for themselves; being a grandparent is not even a part-time job when the grandchildren live a hundred miles away. This is often ill-understood by the younger generation, many of whom still expect grandparents and other old people to stay at home and wait for visitors who only rarely appear. A generation ago it might have been appropriate to take a more passive stance, living life to the dictates of others, but the world has changed and each of us must now take more responsibility for meeting our own needs. Even our way of life precludes most of us from making friends easily as we get older, with neighbours who are often out at work during the day and are unable to spend time chatting. Winter evenings can be a particularly lonely time, for the combination of dark nights, inclement weather and the real, or even imagined, fear of mugging add to the isolation so often experienced. But if we want to remain part of mainstream society, we have to make the effort to go out at least during the day, create our own interests and enjoyment, seek new friends and companions and not be ruled by the opinions or expectations of others.

Taking risks

We have the same rights to self-fulfilment and happiness as the young, even though this may be harder to achieve as the years pass, because we often carry pain and disappointment from the past. This can make us wary of taking risks. We remember old rebuffs or times when we felt foolish or embarrassed by the reaction of others. It is easy to forget that most people are shy and uncertain of themselves. Those who do not talk or offer friendship are usually neither self-confident nor self-sufficient, but have their own uncertainties and are afraid of making the first move for fear of being rejected. There is yet another dilemma which has to be faced as we grow old, for although many of us would like to reap certain of the benefits of ageing, we are reluctant to accept the negative implications that may go with it. Being old encourages a certain amount of deference, such as being helped in getting on and off the bus or having a seat offered to us in the train. But in behaving as though we are 'old' and asking for help in one aspect of daily living, we risk being considered too old to take full responsibility for the rest of our lives and to make our own decisions. We are expected to behave compliantly and conform to stereotypes which we may not like. This may deny us the possibility of exploring new relationships or having an active sex life.

Ageing is lifelong

Ageing is a continuing process, not something we experience as a sudden change which hits us when we reach a certain birthday. Being old is the final part of a journey that starts when we are born and goes on for as long as we live. It is rather like being on a train.

During the first part of the journey as children others take care of us. We absorb knowledge as we go along, looking out of the windows and watching our fellow passengers. During the middle stage, as adults, most of us are fully occupied with travelling arrangements, caring for our families, making certain that we have the tickets, knowing the timetables and having food for the journey. We hardly realise that we have reached the last stage of our journey. What we do notice is that there are fewer people with us and that the travel arrangements seem uncertain. We find ourselves suddenly having to leave the comfortable train and wait on a draughty platform. We wonder whether we have the right tickets. We do not know who is to travel with us, and we are uncertain about the destination.

Coping with change

All through life there are times when we have to cope with change. We have to work out strategies to deal with new situations which are often experienced as a series of losses, such as retirement, or the children leaving home. Another crisis point is the moment of truth when it suddenly dawns on us that our children or other people want to make decisions for us, because they see us as old. We do not recognise that we have begun to age and still think of ourselves as relatively youthful. We want to participate in their activities, while they see this as inappropriate, because they are young and we are not. It is painful to remember that we felt the same about our own parents.

Sex at 70 is good … but it's better if you pull over to the side of the road!

3. Loving and Sexuality

'Old people have the same desires, the same feelings, the same requirements as the young, but the world responds with disgust.'

Simone de Beauvoir

We all need to love and be loved. When we are children or young adults, affection is easier to express. We enjoy physical contact with our partners; we caress our children and we do things for our family, our friends and our parents and so demonstrate that we are loving, caring people. But as we get older and our children and close relatives move away, this physical warmth is more difficult to convey.

Sexuality is a normal part of our make-up as complex human beings, and can enrich our lives and help us at any age to experience new levels of intimacy and personal fulfilment. The ability to feel comfortable and at ease with this fact and use it positively can enhance the whole of life, broaden horizons and harness our energy, giving us access to a degree of happiness and contentment that may not have been possible in earlier years. There is always time to discover new feelings and depths in a relationship. This may even be easier when we have a lifetime's experience behind us.

Younger people's attitudes

Many of today's young people are uncertain about their own sexuality and may be disturbed to think that those who are old or disabled can, and often do, enjoy sex more than they do.

They may also be reluctant to accept that their parents have any sexual feelings. They may rarely see them express physical warmth and may be deeply embarrassed if they are asked to accept a sister or a brother much younger than themselves. It is even more difficult, therefore, for them to accept that their grandparents could also enjoy sexual contact. This applies equally to people who were young fifty years ago and their reluctance to accept this as natural may have stayed with them until the moment when they in turn have to face the reality of their own ageing. If they then experience love or passion, they are likely to be uncomfortable about these feelings, and either try to deny them or else be afraid they are in some way abnormal.

Yet as we age we do not feel differently than we did when we were young. Sometimes we may not be as immediate in our physical or emotional reactions, but we have similar hates and fears and the same capacity to love and to give comfort and support as in we did in our youth.

Sexuality

Some of us worry about losing our sexual potential and powers as we get older, but the majority of these worries are unfounded, as most people are able to enjoy some form of sexual love throughout the whole of life. What is needed is to make the most of the capacity we actually have and adjust to different expressions of sexuality, rather than regret the loss of abilities we might have had when we were young.

We are all to some extent victims of society's wider standards and expectations, which measure and judge people by their performance and success. Anxiety about matching up to imaginary sexual standards may determine how successful we are in our sex lives. We are also often subject to what we think others believe to be acceptable behaviour. This can be very constraining and restrictive.

In our multi-cultural society, views about what is acceptable vary considerably. People should never be persuaded to do anything which offends their own principles nor be prevented from exploring something new in the realms of sexual and personal relationships when they are convinced that it is right for them to do so.

Sex is something that anyone can enjoy although most of us would like to be able to share our pleasure within a permanent relationship. Knowing that we are loved and loveable can be important in giving us confidence and helping to maintain our self-esteem.

Many of us are fortunate in having long-lasting marriages, but whether we are married or not, we all know that our needs vary over the years, as does our capacity to give.

Touching

Sexuality assumes a different importance at different times. As we get older, the intimacy and the touching may be more important than the physical pleasure of intercourse.

We all have a need to touch and be touched both physically and emotionally. Babies need to be handled and caressed in order to develop into adults capable of giving, and receiving, love. It is equally true that adults who lack any form of physical contact with others often shrink within themselves.

As a society we are not very good at touching each other and sadly many old people are never touched, except in a very impersonal way by the doctor or nurse. People are sometimes embarrassed even to see others embracing or holding hands, yet this contact is something we all need. We know that for some the quality of life can be immeasurably improved by keeping a pet, and part of that pleasure lies in the animal's responsiveness to stroking or to the human voice. This can even give a lonely old person a purpose for living.

Mary R had spent much time in hospital due to tuberculosis in early childhood, and rarely saw her parents because of the cost involved in the long journey and the restricted visiting which was usual in those days.

Mary never remembered being hugged by her parents or by her sisters and brothers and as an adult was uncomfortable with any physical contact. She never married.

When she retired from the civil service, she became a volunteer at an old people's day centre. The organiser knew that many older people rarely had opportunities to feel the closeness of another human being and therefore went to a lot of trouble to devise activities like dancing and group exercises, which involved holding hands and linking arms.

Mary was acutely anxious when she realised that she would be drawn into this activity but accepted that, as a helper, she was bound to take part, whether she liked it or not. At first she found this very difficult, but after a while she felt totally at home in the warm and friendly atmosphere of the centre and particularly enjoyed the physical contact with other human beings, which she had never really known.

Intimacy

For many couples, the shared intimacy of body contact, the opportunity of lying next to each other, of stroking, touching, caressing, and of being held, can be more important than the genital excitement of a sexual relationship. It offers reassurance and comfort, an opportunity to show love and tenderness, and to whisper of the joys and fears that are rarely spoken about in the cold light of day.

Intimacy is a very special part of a relationship. It involves an emotional touching in which we expose some small part of ourselves to another person. It may happen when we see a film, listen to music or watch television with a friend. A feeling is stirred and we realise that this is shared. We each allow ourselves to be vulnerable and trust the other person. This experience of trust is central to any loving relationship.

Most of us live the largest part of our lives on a very superficial level. We talk about the weather, the news and the family in a cautious way and are reluctant to share our most private feelings with strangers, acquaintances or even friends, for fear that through exposing something deeply personal to others, our vulnerability will be abused.

Intimacy, that rare and valued touching of feelings, can happen when we share any deep experience and also when we make love, for the nakedness of intercourse is not only physical, but sometimes a deep emotional nakedness as well, which brings us into real contact with another person and at that moment we know we are not alone. In allowing ourselves to take risks within a loving relationship, we become more loveable.

The emotional, social, physical and spiritual components of life are all so closely interwoven that it is difficult for most people to separate them from each other. The majority would like sex to be a reflection of a total relationship which has all these components, but for others it can be a purely physical experience and bring its own rewards and relief of tension. We need to accept these differences and not be critical of those whose behaviour differs from our own.

Most people do not talk about their feelings when making love, but slip into using gestures and touch to express physically the love and the reassurance that they sometimes cannot put into words.

Sexuality is an important dimension in our lives irrespective of age. It affects our relationships with others as well as reinforcing our own feelings of self-esteem and worth.

Changes over time

Sex is a powerful instinct, and orgasm, shared or alone, can bring overwhelming feelings of pleasure and contentment. Sexual behaviour among couples varies considerably over time. Sometimes there is a great deal of passion; at others there are calmer, quieter episodes. Experiences change throughout life together, and in one relationship there may be periods when sex becomes less necessary or even burdensome. This is not a reason for accusing one partner of being frigid or impotent, any more than apportioning blame at times of increased sexual needs. Desire varies according to a range of factors, from physical health and emotional well-being to worries about family, work or money.

It is normal for there to be fluctuations and changes, but a prerequisite of a good relationship is the ability to adapt to each other's needs and to ensure that it is not always the same partner who has to make the adjustments. Many women still feel that their husbands should initiate sex while men sometimes wish that they did not always have to be the more active partner but cannot communicate this to their wives.

The sexual act may be more difficult for men because it is linked to potent performance and the ability to maintain an erection, whereas women can enjoy their feelings until such a time as they are ready to come to orgasm or even in its absence.

For many older women the fact that their husbands may now take longer to reach a climax is a bonus. It makes love-making far more enjoyable than when they travelled along that particular road at a speed reminiscent of a racing car accelerating from 0 to 80mph in seconds. It may cause men anxiety and regret to have slowed down, but this apparent inadequacy can be turned to advantage, giving time for both partners to explore new sensations and enjoy the variety of feelings that more prolonged intercourse can give.

Until quite recently sex, for many women, was intentionally limited to their child-bearing years. If their sex life had been unsatisfactory, the arrival of the menopause was a time when, with some relief, they could say 'that's the end of it' and discontinue sex completely.

The attitudes of many women towards sex were epitomised by the mother who told her daughter on the eve of her wedding, 'close your eyes and think of England'. Men, conversely, may have been more influenced by the Victorian gentleman who firmly told his second wife on their honeymoon, 'ladies don't move'.

It is probably only within the last thirty years, with safe contraception and a re-evaluation of women's role in society, that we have been able to shake ourselves free of the attitudes which maintained that sex was for the enjoyment of men and that women preferred motherhood and caring for children and husbands. We now realise that the pleasure women get from sex depends on their own determination and freedom to enjoy sexual pleasure and the willingness of their chosen partner to co-operate and care.

We also know that women have at least the same capacity as men to enjoy sex, plus the additional advantage for many of retaining their ability to have several orgasms one after another until much later in life. Men, however, though capable of making love several times a night when they are young, may, as they get older, be satisfied with sexual activity only once or twice a week or even much less.

4. Understanding Attitudes to Sexuality

'I refuse to admit that I am more than 52 even if that does make my sons illegitimate.'

Nancy, Lady Astor

S ome of the problems that older people have to cope with nowadays result from attitudes that were prevalent during their formative years which assigned very different social and sexual roles to men and to women. These have to be understood and put into perspective so that older men and women can make choices that are appropriate to the way they wish to live now.

O lder women

Women who grew up before the Second World War generally expected little pleasure from sex. They were taught that outside marriage it was both sinful and dangerous and even when they married, they did not expect to be sexually fulfilled. This was compounded by the widespread fear among men that their own sexual performance might be at risk if they attempted to please their wives in love-making. So women were excluded from the pleasures of sex, just as they were from pubs and clubs. Few wives expected their husbands to satisfy their sexual needs and often experienced a sense of deep guilt and anxiety that they might be abnormal even to have such feelings.

Fear of pregnancy

It was commonly believed that conception would not occur if the woman remained passive and unaroused during intercourse and many women were, of course, anxious to limit the size of their family. If husbands were also going to blame unwanted pregnancies on their wives, because they wanted sexual pleasure, marital relationships were unlikely to be very enjoyable, and until family planning advice became widely available in the 1950s and '60s, these fears were always in the background.

Talk about sexuality fifty years ago was tolerated only within strictly laid down boundaries. Men would exchange details of their conquests and their pleasures, either real or imaginary. Women in general shared unpleasant experiences. Some hated sex so much that they even went as far as neglecting their appearance, unconsciously using their lack of attractiveness as a way of discontinuing unwanted sexual advances by their husbands.

It is not surprising that women who had consistently bad sexual experiences used the menopause as an excuse to ensure that their sex life ceased, although those women who did find satisfaction were, in general, pleased to be able to continue love-making without the use of contraceptives. Older women who enjoy sex rarely call a halt to that part of a marital relationship and women who lose their partner through death, divorce or separation and are left alone, do not necessarily lose their need for sex and sexual satisfaction.

A new partner

Finding a new partner is particularly difficult for older women, for not only are they far more numerous than older men, but men of their own age are often looking for much younger partners. Women may feel embarrassed about trying to find partners younger than themselves for fear of being thought of as 'cradle-snatchers' or worse.

Society as reflected by the media finds it perfectly acceptable for a man to marry a much younger woman, but an older woman married to a younger man is often regarded as a figure of fun and ridicule. Of course it is possible in either type of relationship for the younger person to be interested only in tangible rewards, but it is just as feasible for an older woman and a younger man to enjoy a mutually satisfactory marriage as for any other couple.

Girls expect to marry men older than themselves and this ensures that most men get cared for when they are old by their younger wives, while older women are rarely cared for by their partners. With women on the whole living considerably longer than men, it would shorten the lonely years of widowhood if more women married younger men.

Loss

As they get older, women are often deeply affected by a string of losses: the loss of their job as they approach retirement age, of their children as they leave home, of their own parents as they die or become frail and dependent, and very often the irreparable loss of their husband if they are widowed. When these losses occur in middle age, they are often accepted as the inevitable lot of women, and not worked through or understood, and consequently cause major problems later.

As emotional attachments are so important to a woman, the end of a close, loving relationship through death or separation can have a double effect. She is likely to have made an enormous emotional investment in the relationship and will lose a part of herself as well as her husband when he dies. On the other hand, if her marriage was not successful, she may see herself as a total failure and her life as meaningless when it ends through his death.

Search for youthfulness

For many women their own ageing may be one of the most difficult things that they have to accept and they may feel obliged to pursue what they see as a youthful image at all costs. This can be searching in vain and what is intended to appear youthful from their point of view may be perceived by others as inappropriate or even grotesque. Older women can, and do, radiate charm, beauty and personality in their own right but, because of the way beauty in the young is so often considered the norm, many feel ageing to be one of the greatest disasters they face. This is reinforced by their image as reflected in dramas and books and by advertising in newspapers, magazines and on television, which seem to disqualify them from normal social life.

Most women, especially those who are now elderly, were brought up to conform to a pattern in which they had to please and attract men, and they often experience ageing as a form of punishment and humiliation.

Older men are frequently considered attractive and very eligible, but this is rare for older women. For many women, the most important power they ever had was to attract men sexually and with the disappearance of that power, their hope of any future happiness also fades. One danger is that they can as a result be so overwhelmed with loss and grief that they get very depressed. This in turn leads them to withdraw from mainstream society and reinforces their feeling of uselessness.

Our vision of beauty should be broader and not restricted to physical attributes. The beauty to be looked for in both older women and men is a reflection of their warmth and energy and their empathy towards other people.

Strength of character and experience are often qualities attributed to older men but they apply to women as well. There is also much beauty to be found in relationships between people.

Lesbians are a minority group who have often experienced difficulties in finding agencies and individuals with the knowledge and experience to help them when they are in difficulty. This is particularly true of older lesbians, but their situation is now gradually beginning to improve although they have been doubly discriminated against in the past.

The women's movement, which has done a great deal to help women to be more assertive and confident about their needs both at a personal and a social level, has tended until very recently to concentrate its efforts on younger women and to disregard their older sisters.

The liberation of older women is only just beginning, but they must identify what they want to change in their own lives, and not simply wait to be liberated by others.

Women in a more active role

Many of today's younger women are now more assertive, expressing their feelings and needs to their partners by telling them precisely what they want and enjoy in love-making. Those now in their sixties or older, many of whom have been brought up to believe that sexuality was primarily for the pleasure of men, now have the chance to put the record straight. They have the opportunity both to have their own needs met and sometimes to adopt the more active role in love-making.

Most older women are happy to take a more active role but can only do this within the security of a long lasting partnership. Others are able to enjoy sex as a physical pleasure irrespective of the nature of the relationship.

*I*sabel and Ronald M had been married for 35 years. Isabel rarely experienced orgasm through intercourse. She was able to masturbate and reach a climax, but although her husband stimulated her clitoris with his hand to get her excited at the beginning of love-making, he went on to vaginal intercourse too quickly for her to climax. The vaginal stimulation was never enough in itself to bring her to orgasm. Gradually she became disinterested in sex, even though she felt obliged to meet her husband's needs.

One evening they watched a TV counselling programme. The discussion was about the difficulty many women have in asking for what they want sexually. Ronald commented that he couldn't understand any woman not being able to say what she enjoyed. As a result, Isabel found herself able to confess to him that she had never been able to say such things and had always asked for what she thought he wanted. Ronald managed to reassure his wife that he really wanted to please her. Their sex life began to improve and he found that through enjoying her increased pleasure, his own sex life was better too.*

Differing Needs

We all differ in our needs. For some of us sexuality has always been an important driving force. For others it is much less important. Although the presence of a loved one may make us more conscious of our sexuality, we do not necessarily lose our sexual feelings just because we do not have a partner.

Many people who are now in their seventies or eighties were brought up at a time when masturbation was considered not only a sin, but also as a potential hazard leading to mental illness, infertility and moral degeneration. Although these misconceptions have been left behind, the feelings generated still remain, with the result that many older people find it difficult to give themselves pleasure without overwhelming sensations of guilt.

This is sad, for the joy of sex, and the relief of sexual tension, can be a source of pleasure for everyone and people should be free to decide for themselves what they need and what is right for them personally.

Everybody is subject to certain constraints. Some are based on a realistic assessment of what an ageing body can do. Others reflect the type of society we live in. Yet others are dreamed up by people who have no real idea of the feelings and needs of those who are older.

For many years it has been tacitly accepted, rightly or wrongly, that men's sexual needs are not necessarily only satisfied within marriage. Women should similarly give some thought to the expression of their own needs and make choices that are appropriate for them. They do not automatically have to accept rules and standards that were laid down for a very different society, although most will find it difficult and unsuitable to consider alternatives and will only want to express sexuality within marriage.

Sexual identity

This also applies to sexual identity. Most people are attracted by members of the opposite sex; some people can only love others of the same sex. A very large number of people are capable of both heterosexual and homosexual love.

As we age, our circles of friends and acquaintances get smaller and because women tend to live longer than men, it may be difficult for them to find a friend or a partner of the opposite sex.

Many people feel more comfortable and less pressured with the companionship, friendship and love of someone of their own sex. They may also find that they are able to express with a friend warmth and tenderness and physical affection that enrich their lives and this may extend to a close sexual relationship.

Patricia F and Alison J had been close friends for many years and always showed their affection for each other by warmly embracing when they met. After they were both widowed they went on holiday together and sharing a bed found that they could give each other sexual pleasure. Their relationship continued for many years and no-one questioned their obvious warmth and love for each other.

This is probably easier for women than it is for men, as our culture allows women to demonstrate affection openly. The love of two women is usually accepted by society without assumptions being made about the nature of their relationship.

Harry L and Michael S had enjoyed a stable relationship for 20 years. When Harry could no longer manage to live at home because of the care he needed, he went into hospital. Michael visited him regularly and when they sat and held hands the other patients and staff seemed outraged.

The love and affection two people have for each other brings with it a warmth which is of value in its own right, and it is sad when the positive aspects of such relationships are denied.

Our way of life is usually determined by strongly held religious or ethical principles, but we may find that over the years our feelings change. If this happens we should not be afraid or ashamed to make choices, provided that we know these choices are right for us.

Older Men

The past twenty years have seen such an upsurge of interest in the problems of women that it is very easy for men to feel ignored and discriminated against. They might well question the widely held belief that men have always had the best side of the bargain and that life is automatically much easier for those born male.

Most would probably agree that, until quite recently, in some ways they certainly did fare better than women, but even so there were drawbacks.

The role of men in the past

Admittedly, men were traditionally the hunters, able to ask girls for dates, to take the initiative at dances and decide who to kiss or grope. That was fine for men who were sure of themselves, but not so good for those who were shy and uncertain, or not very skilled at saying the right thing at the right time.

Most men who are now retired were children at a time when the average male worked very long hours, six days a week. Many were brought up to believe that a man should be the main breadwinner and master of the house, and that when he came home he should be looked after and waited on by his wife and daughters. They also assumed that women enjoyed looking after the house, even if they too went out to work.

Although some men had begun to change their attitudes slightly, occasionally doing the washing up and accompanying their wives on the weekly trip to the shops, they felt resentful when they assisted with their chores, and found their efforts criticised and undervalued. If they heard their wives complaining they tended to think that this was one of the inevitable irritations of married life, rather than believing that it might be based on a real sense of injustice.

THE WOMEN'S MOVEMENT

Men probably found it quite difficult to understand what was happening when they found themselves confronted by a Women's Movement which campaigned about the exploitation of women, their lack of choice and lack of status. As seen through the eyes of many men, women had 'never had it so good'. Certainly their lives were much easier than those of their mothers, with labour-saving appliances and far more time for leisure. Surely they had wanted to get married and have children and settle down? So what had gone wrong? Hardly surprisingly, the Women's Movement must have seemed to many men to be set on making women who had previously been content with their lot, discontented and unhappy.

Increasingly, too, men found they were expected to help with the children and the cleaning. Those who had been brought up by mothers whose world revolved around looking after husband, family and home, must have found it confusing, sometimes even upsetting to realise that their wives had other interests.

Problems of performance

This confusion in social roles was mirrored in bed. For those same men had learnt about sex at a time when it was genuinely believed that men were sexually more active than women, that men should always be the initiators and that they had more need of sexual satisfaction than their wives.

Of course many men realised that women could be responsive and had the need for satisfaction when aroused, but the idea that women had sexual needs unrelated to those of men was relatively unknown and rarely acknowledged.

It is easy to blame men for this appalling lack of sensitivity, but the myth that was widely, and undoubtedly conveniently, accepted was that while men had sexual needs, women's needs were to be wives and mothers, giving satisfaction to those around them and not asking much in return.

Myths are retained if they are useful and this particular myth not only gave men permission to seek and accept sexual satisfaction for themselves, but also a convenient alibi if their wives failed to respond to their advances.

The virile husband is supposed to be always ready for sex, and able to produce an erection at will and, not surprisingly, many men find this schoolboy fantasy difficult to live up to. It then becomes convenient for them to fall back on the excuse of their wife's failure to respond, rather than trying to resolve the conflict between the level of performance they ought to attain and the reality of what they can manage.

The anxiety generated by this inability to match up to their own internal standards may be aggravated by an increasingly wide understanding of the sexual needs of women. If men are no longer able to blame their wives for unsatisfactory sexual intercourse, they may have to accept that they do not match up to their own expectations of a 'real' man. Some men can only resolve this conflict by giving up sex altogether.

As men age, their sexual needs tend to lessen and by the time they reach their seventies, they do not have as hard an erection as when they were younger. Spontaneous erection, too, occurs far less frequently, while some men find it difficult to produce an erection even with stimulation.

This may be yet another problem for the man who is used to being the initiator and taking the more active role. He may be very embarrassed to find that his erection is no longer hard enough to achieve penetration.

Advice

Another problem for men is that women traditionally have more access to advice than they have. Women usually take their children to doctors when they are ill or need inoculations and get to know them better. They may be more comfortable than men in asking for advice.

They may also be the ones who are in contact with the Citizens' Advice Bureau or social services and are therefore able to mention their own difficulties in passing, hoping that their needs will be recognised and met, whereas men often have to make a special visit to these agencies for help and are uncertain whether it is even appropriate for them to do so.

So men are often left to cope with their own emotional problems, with no-one to consult other than work mates and friends.

'Better to stick to someone you know, Maud – so soon after your heart attack!'

5. *Facing Sexual Difficulties*

'Few people know how to be old.'

La Rochefoucauld

*A*lthough we know that there are some septuagenarians climbing mountains and running marathons, most of us begin to notice some slowing down in our bodies as we age, and the tasks that used to be finished before we started work now often seem to take the whole morning to complete. This applies to sex as much as to other parts of life. One elderly gentleman said rather regretfully, 'It now takes all night to do what I used to do all night'.

*G*eneral Health Problems

As well as these general feelings, many of us also begin to experience more specific complaints that interfere with the quality of life and our ability to enjoy sex. Sometimes we go to the doctor for help, but often we put up with discomfort, rather than make a fuss. Sexual difficulties and problems cannot all be solved, but they can often be helped by quite minor adjustments, if both partners are willing to try.

Pain

Sex is something to be enjoyed. This may be difficult if every movement causes pain, or if joints and limbs cannot be moved because of stiffness and discomfort. Even the fear that something might be painful will prevent sexual arousal, if experience has shown that the pain that is felt is not compensated for by the pleasure gained. Arthritis is a problem that often comes with ageing, and can be extremely painful. Sometimes the pain is constant and nagging. It may be exacerbated by moving suddenly and may affect the range of movement a joint can make.

Arthritis of the hip is extremely common, and although many people have been cured by joint replacement, there are still many thousands who find that the pain of arthritis not only restricts all normal tasks but also prevents any sexual activity.

This may be a particular difficulty for women, for one of the earliest symptoms of arthritis in the hip is an inability to open the legs or rotate the hip. It may make intercourse in the more usual postures, with the woman lying on her back, totally impossible.

*A*nne and John B had been married for 40 years and had always enjoyed sex. During the past five years Anne had become increasingly disabled by her arthritic hip. This didn't cause a great deal of pain when walking, but she found that she could not separate her legs for intercourse. She and John had always had sex with Anne on her back and John lying on top of her and they were both afraid of trying a new position. They were not able to tell their doctor how much the arthritis was affecting the quality of their sex life and, after Anne had a hip replacement operation, were afraid of seeking advice from their surgeon, so they stopped sex completely because they were worried about damaging the new hip joint. Eventually John plucked up courage to ask the surgeon if Anne's new hip joint was at risk and was relieved to hear that as three months had now elapsed since the operation, normal activity, including sex, would not cause damage.

Sometimes the problem of pain can be overcome by using a different position. One way is for the woman to lie on her side, with her partner lying behind her 'like a pair of spoons'.

Changing position will also help those couples who have painful knees, backs or shoulders and cannot cope with weight-bearing or bending arthritic joints.

The use of pillows to support and cushion painful limbs and stop unnecessary movement will also help. If a pillow is not firm or long enough, use a bolster or a rolled up blanket for support. Many women or men lying on their back, with their partner on top, find that a pillow in the small of the back can both give support and increase their pleasure.

Pain can, of course, be overcome by taking adequate doses of pain killers, preferably before foreplay commences. Most pain killers take

10-15 minutes fully to take effect, so they should be kept by the bedside and used at the first sign of sexual activity. This will enormously enhance the enjoyment of both partners and even if it all fizzles out and nothing happens, an extra dose of pain killer will not do any harm.

Being warm in bed also helps alleviate pain, and keeping hands under the covers if the room is not very warm may make love-making for both partners more pleasant. Cold and painful arthritic fingers will not be able to give pleasure, and fingers are important in receiving sensation. The feeling of a warm, responsive body that is sexually aroused is an important part of sexual enjoyment.

All these suggestions need practice and perseverance, so no-one should be put off because something doesn't work on the first occasion. Sex should be fun, and failure or difficulties in trying new positions and new techniques should be a cue for laughter, and not a matter of concern or a sign of failure.

A few people get pain in the chest during intercourse, which only eases when sexual activity stops. This should be reported to the doctor, who will prescribe treatment for this condition.

Drugs and medicines

It is important to remember that some prescribed medicines affect sexual performance and the full enjoyment of intercourse. Some affect a man's ability to get or maintain an erection; others may prevent him reaching a climax. Some just act as a turn-off, taking away all sexual feelings. Certain drugs are very likely to have such an effect and usually doctors explain this. Occasionally the tablets or medicines may be 'selective' and affect some people and not others. Doctors are some-times reluctant to list all the possible side-effects of a drug for fear they might put ideas into people's minds. This may or may not be true, but all side-effects should be reported and the doctor told of any sexual problems that may arise, for it is often possible to change the treatment.

Sometimes, though, a treatment will inevitably interfere with sexual performance. Most people would probably not want to take risks with their health in order to continue with sexual activity, but some feel that the quality of life is more important than the chance of a few extra years, and refuse treatment that interferes with sexual enjoyment. Doctors and patients should discuss both the dangers and the difficulties together, so that patients can make a fully informed choice as to whether they wish to continue with such treatment.

Fortunately, increasing numbers of doctors are becoming aware that drugs can have these effects. They are also realising that sex is an important part of life for many older couples, who must decide for themselves whether they wish to take a particular form of treatment or not.

Urinary incontinence

By the time they are 50, almost 50 per cent of women occasionally suffer from some form of urinary incontinence. Many men are also affected. Yet it is one of the most difficult things to acknowledge and so people are very reluctant to seek help. This is sad because a great deal can be done to improve the condition and to remove the embarrassment it creates. Stress incontinence is particularly common and can be brought on by sudden coughing, laughing or sneezing, causing uncontrolled spurts of urine.

This type of incontinence may be due to a variety of factors such as a sudden increase or decrease in weight and, in women, the stretching of the pelvic muscles during childbirth. It can also be due to urinary infections. Special exercises can help to strengthen lax muscles and urinating and stopping the flow every few moments is simple and often effective and should be practised occasionally by all people in later life. There are also small devices which can be worn inside the vagina by women to help to improve muscular tone.

Another form of incontinence affects people who normally manage quite comfortably to go for hours without a visit to the lavatory, and who then find that they have a sudden uncontrollable urge as they reach their own front door.

It is important to change underwear frequently and keep clean. It may be particularly embarrassing if incontinence occurs during intercourse. The best way of coping with this is to empty the bladder before going to bed and before starting to make love, and to refrain from drinking in the two to three hours before bedtime. Lying on a small towel during intercourse may help to give reassurance and if there is any spillage will prevent the bedclothes being soiled.

Faecal incontinence

This is far less frequent but can be a serious problem for some people. To prevent it happening it is important to try to empty the bowel before going to bed. If this is impossible to do easily, it is worth using a suppository earlier in the evening or even having a regular enema. This will keep the lower bowel empty and ensure that there is no spillage during sex. Some people worry about having an accident, and if this is likely, special incontinence pants with appropriate apertures can be worn during intercourse.

Continence advisors will be able to give individual advice. (See *Seeking Help and Advice*.) Some older people find that they get a type of diarrhoea, which occurs after one or two days' constipation. This should be reported to the doctor as it may be a symptom of something more serious.

Catheters

Some people have to wear catheters and are worried that they will interfere with intercourse but they need not cause excessive difficulties. The bladder should be emptied before going to bed. Men can strap their catheter back with adhesive plaster along the penis while women can strap the end of theirs to the thigh. In this way catheters will hardly be noticed during intercourse, nor will they be damaged and most people find them quite unobtrusive. Some people change their catheters themselves, and can remove them for intercourse and reinsert them afterwards.

Breathlessness

Breathlessness may occur because of anaemia, obesity, heart or circulation problems, asthma or diminished lung function. It may follow an illness which is being treated, or may arise for the first time quite unexpectedly during sexual intercourse, but it should be reported to the doctor.

If breathlessness is a problem during intercourse, it is advisable to use techniques which diminish the effort. The breathless partner should not take the more active weight-bearing role.

The use of a vibrator or dildo (see page 85) may help a man pleasure his wife without expending too much energy or becoming too breathless and this may also be avoided by being propped up in bed rather than lying flat. Making love sitting in a chair is another option and it may be easier to spend more time on foreplay and caressing, enjoying the pleasures of closeness, warmth and loving, without having to achieve a climax each time.

Heart attacks

As people live longer, they are more likely to suffer from some deterioration in their cardiac efficiency and some people get 'heart attacks'. Twenty or thirty years ago they would have expected to spend the rest of their life as a cardiac invalid. Nowadays, however, people are encouraged to return to full activity as soon as possible. Generally it is accepted that anyone who can walk up two flights of stairs can easily manage sexual intercourse, and as sex is an enjoyable activity, it should be resumed as soon as the couple wish.

The strain of lying in bed, wanting sex, yet being afraid of the damage that it may cause, may be far more dangerous than anything that may happen during intercourse itself. Comfortable sex with a familiar partner is also therapeutic.

Doctors may have reservations about the advisability of having sex with a new partner after a heart attack – not because of any moral judgement, but because the anxiety about performance or undue excitement are factors that can cause heart strain.

When sexual activity is resumed after a heart attack it should be as gentle and undemanding as possible. Patients should lie on their back or on their side and not take the extra strain of weight-bearing. Sexual activity need not necessarily go to orgasm, though it should not be stopped because of fear of over-exertion. Use of vibrators or dildos may make love-making less of an effort.

Strokes

This word, like cancer, seems to have an ominous and final ring about it, but treatment has radically changed over the last few years and many people are still able to live full and independent lives after quite severe strokes.

A stroke affects one side of the body only and produces weakness and paralysis in the arm and leg to varying degrees. If the right side of the body is affected, speech may be impaired. A stroke is often accompanied by diminished coordination, and reading may also be affected through partial blindness which makes it difficult to read the beginning or end of a line.

An added problem is that a stroke is often accompanied by severe depression, and this may prevent the patient from being able to muster enough initiative to try to overcome the subsequent disabilities.

People who have had a stroke are liable to believe that life is over for them. They can't imagine that they will be able in future to do anything either for themselves or for others. Somebody has to work very hard to combat this apparent inertia in order to activate, encourage and force them into rehabilitating themselves. Helping them to enjoy sex again and to give sexual pleasure to their partner may be an important step in this rehabilitation.

*G*eoff T *was very depressed after his stroke and felt trapped by his clumsy body. He would have liked to have had sex but was desperately afraid that any unusual activity would bring on another* *attack and leave him permanently disabled. Geoff's wife, Rita had to do almost everything for him. He knew that she didn't mind, but he wanted to show his appreciation and love. She had always been a highly-sexed woman who had enjoyed love-making and he was afraid that his present inactivity was a real deprivation for her. He spoke to his doctor about this and the doctor suggested getting a vibrator and using it together. Geoff was delighted and found that in giving Rita pleasure he became sexually aroused and was able to enjoy gentle love-making. His doctor had assured him that this was no risk to his health. Geoff was surprised to find how much better life seemed.*

Depression

Everyone becomes depressed at some time in their lives. It is a normal reaction to loss. The loss may be of a significant person through death or divorce, a child leaving home, or someone special going to live far away. Depression may also be caused by loss of status or shortage of money, either of which might follow retirement or redundancy, or be due to disability or the realisation that with ageing, activities and opportunities are beginning to narrow.

Sometimes the depression is transitory but it can become chronic and a way of life, so that many older people are continually depressed, miserable and under par.

Depression affects people differently. Some lose their appetite, others eat abnormally. Some will sleep badly, waking early in the morning and being restless at night. Others will sleep most of the day away. Sometimes depression can be severe enough to mimic dementia.

An early symptom of depression, and one which is often neglected and ignored, is the loss of sexual drive. Without an understanding of this, many people believe it to be a symptom of ageing rather than an illness which can be cured.

Because depression is often thought of as inevitable, many people do not bother to try to get treatment. There are however anti-depressant treatments that can be prescribed, which are often very effective. Counselling, by providing an opportunity to identify and examine the nature of the problems, can be of immense help.

Dementia

Dementia, most frequently in the form of Alzheimer's Disease, is a condition that is usually associated with old age. It has been estimated that 20 per cent of people over 80 suffer from some degree of dementia, though this can often be very mild and never progress beyond failing memory and slight confusion. It is quite different from the forgetfulness that attacks many of us at various stages of our lives and which can be counteracted by memory techniques and by trying harder to remember the things that are really important.

While the majority of us will survive into old age with our mental faculties intact, a significant minority will not and for most this condition is particularly dreaded because of the loss of dignity that seems to accompany it. As with many other things that we dread, it may be that, should it actually happen to us, life would not be nearly as bad as we imagine. However this does not solve the problem of coping with the early stages of this illness ourselves or with watching someone we love slowly deteriorate.

Fortunately there are now organisations and individuals who can be of immense help when it comes to coping with this situation and offering support. (See *Seeking Help and Advice*.)

One of the things that must be remembered, however, is that the brain has a habit of compensating for much that goes wrong, and people may be able to retain the ability to live a fairly full life. Personal relationships and sexual behaviour could even change for the better, with the onset of dementia, when some lifelong inhibitions might be released. This needs to be understood with sensitivity by partners and by others who are involved in the caring process.

Operations

Any surgical operation can have a devastating effect on the older person, for the psychological upheaval can be as exhausting as the physical trauma.

It may take many weeks before the patient feels well again, for older bodies take longer to recover fully from operations and anaesthetics, and the recovery period requires more rest than usual. Simple household tasks become tiring and everything seems to take much longer than before.

Another problem is that an operation, if not actually life saving itself, is very often concerned with halting a potentially life threatening condition. It can, therefore, create psychological or even spiritual upheaval as people confront the possibility of their own death, perhaps for the first time. Any of these personal crises can affect sexual feelings and performance.

This is particularly true of operations on 'private parts', such as penis, testicles or prostate in a man, or vulva, vagina or uterus in a woman.

Many people are afraid that sexual intercourse, after such an operation, will either damage the patient, or possibly be the cause of an unpleasant infection or disease in the partner.

These fears are quite understandable although nearly always unjustified, but they may be the cause of considerable marital distress and disharmony at a time when the support and comfort of intimacy are most needed.

Most couples need the help of a counsellor or social worker to work through the anxieties that these operations may generate, and they should not be afraid to ask for help, if none is offered.

It is important for patients and their partners to be fully informed of all the possible consequences of any operation. Patients have to sign a consent form and it is reasonable to ask for clarification about any point that is worrying or not understood. Obtaining informed consent is part of a doctor's duty and this includes a responsibility to provide adequate information.

The trauma of an operation can affect sexual responsiveness; and some couples imagine that because things have temporarily changed, sexual feelings will never return.

*P*aul K had always been proud of being able to satisfy his wife, *Jane sexually. After his hernia operation he felt weak and depressed. To his dismay he found that he had lost all sexual feeling and was sorry for his wife so tried for her sake to become sexually aroused. His small erection disappeared as soon as he tried to penetrate her. This happened every time over a few weeks and Paul became ashamed of his inability to perform and felt he was letting Jane down. Sex had always been something they had enjoyed but never spoken about. He pretended to fall asleep. Jane realised that there were many things that Paul was unable to do after the operation and she assumed that this was one of them. So she held him lovingly and suggested that it would be better to wait a little longer before trying to have intercourse. As Paul's general health got better he found that his former potency was gradually restored.*

After operations when people feel low, they need more than ever the reassurance that they are still loved. The closeness of lying together, of feeling protected and cared for, may do more good than a doctor's prescription. Very often, it is in these private, quiet moments together in the darkness that a couple can share their fears and anxieties and reassure each other that they are loved and valued.

All operations tend to be frightening. Most people do not like going into hospital and nearly everyone is scared of anaesthetics, but there are some operations that, because of their nature, are more likely to interfere with sexual function than others.

Prostate operation

The prostate is a gland at the base of the bladder, and if it becomes enlarged it can interfere with a man's enjoyment of sex.

Sometimes the pressure of an enlarged prostate can increase sexual feelings and some men are embarrassed because they find themselves becoming sexually aroused at unusual times. They may get pain in the penis or find difficulty in maintaining an erection or reaching a climax. They may also find that their partners become frustrated by a continually unsatisfactory sexual relationship unless they are particularly sensitive to this. Sometimes such problems can be helped by using a sex aid, which relieves the pressure on the man to perform beyond his capacity.

Many men find that their sexual responses are unchanged after surgical treatment, but some find their libido, the desire for sex, becomes less, and when they do have intercourse, they produce less fluid on ejaculation and the intensity of feeling at the time of orgasm is not as strong as it was before.

Surgeons should explain this before the operation, and partners, too, should be told of this possible outcome. If it is not discussed, problems can arise because the wife feels sexually frustrated, or may even believe that her husband is purposely withholding satisfaction.

Cancer of the prostate gland

This is sometimes treated by orchidectomy, the surgical removal of the testicles. The operation which is usually very successful in the treatment of the cancer, results in the loss of sexual feeling.

Amputation of the penis

Cancer of the penis may necessitate amputation of all or part of the penis and after convalescence the husband may want some form of sexual activity to recommence. This can be very upsetting if the couple have not had adequate counselling and an opportunity to share their anxieties, as well as to get sufficient reassurance that sexual activity is not harmful.

Colostomy

A colostomy is an operation in which a portion of intestine is brought to the surface to open on the abdominal wall. The opening may be fitted with a cap to prevent spillage, or may open into a special colostomy bag that has to be emptied from time to time. This can be very embarrassing, even though a colostomy is usually performed as a life-saving measure. Most people manage to accept this radical change in their body image, although many find it extremely distasteful.

It is sometimes tempting to move to separate rooms after this type of operation because of embarrassment about the bag or a possible unpleasant odour. Once this happens, however, it may be difficult to find the right time to resume sharing.

The colostomy is no reason in itself to abstain from sex, although it may take some time after such a major operation to feel well enough to engage in any normal activity. It is never too soon, however, for the couple to revert to the gentle physical closeness of touching and caressing.

Whether sex resumes for a couple after a colostomy operation depends on their previous sexual relationship and also on the degree of intimacy they have and their ability to talk about emotional difficulties and needs.

It also partly depends on the help they are given by the hospital. There is an organisation of specially trained nurses who visit most patients in hospital after a colostomy operation. They will help them cope with the problems that may arise at home, and will usually raise the topic of sex, although they may sometimes wait for the subject to be broached. It is important to find out about these specialist nurses.

It requires a lot of sensitivity to reassure anyone who has had a colostomy that he or she is still loved and loveable, and the well partner may need support from the doctor, hospital or ostomy association to make sure that this happens. Some people find that instead of being ashamed of their colostomy bag, they cope by making it a feature and making themselves decorative bags to cover it.

Coronary by-pass

A coronary by-pass operation is intended to restore heart activity to normal or near-normal, after a heart attack or the threat of one. Doctors will give individual advice and will suggest the time when sexual activity to orgasm can be recommenced, but this is usually about four to six weeks after the operation, and is related to the ability to walk upstairs without pain or breathlessness.

Mastectomy

The removal of a breast, which is usually done because of cancer, is not as mutilating an operation as it was a few years ago. It may still, however, be a particularly difficult operation for women, and their partners, to accept.

Because our first experience of being nurtured is connected with our mothers' breasts, they have a deep psychological significance, reflected in the sexual symbolism associated with them. Therefore if a woman loses a breast, either in part or in its entirety, this is likely to have a devastating effect on her and on her partner.

Many women feel mutilated and unfeminine, afraid to let their partner see the result of the operation. Some do not realise in advance that they are likely to lose a breast, thinking that they are only about to have an exploratory operation, and wake up to find that the breast has been amputated. This should normally not happen for women and their partners should have such a possibility clearly spelled out to them in advance of signing the consent form. Nowadays there is a wide variety of appropriate procedures other than total mastectomy for treating cancer of the breast and patients should ask about them before consenting to any one form of treatment.

Unfortunately many surgeons, thinking only of the physical well-being of their patient, do not take any account of her relationship with her partner. Some surgical departments, however, do have social workers or counsellors whose task is to discuss the operation with both partners, giving them an opportunity to talk about their feelings. They will also talk about sex, suggesting ways in which it can be resumed as soon as possible.

Hysterectomy

The operation of hysterectomy, the removal of the uterus or womb, is usually performed on women in their forties and fifties, but it is sometimes recommended for older women. The uterus in the post-menopausal woman is about the size of a small tangerine and is located at the top of the vagina. The neck of the womb, the cervix, which is like a small knob, protrudes into the upper end of the vagina, and can usually be quite easily felt. Many women who have used a contraceptive cap have been taught to feel its position to make sure that the cap is correctly in place. Many men have felt this knob when exploring their partner's vagina and will know that moving it gently is, for most women sexually exciting.

Women's feelings about their uterus are very complicated, as it is so closely linked to periods and pregnancy, femininity and youth. Although most women over the age of sixty have little practical use for the uterus, they may have deep psychological anxieties about having it removed. Because women of this age are no longer fertile, many doctors do not spend time in explanations, with the result that husbands and wives may be left to cope with strange or unpleasant fantasies, because they do not know enough anatomy to reassure themselves.

The operation for removing the uterus may be performed by an incision through the abdominal muscles, in which case there is a visible scar, or it may be taken away through the vagina and leave no scar. In either case the vagina is usually left intact and the operation will not interfere with sexual enjoyment although very occasionally it may entail some shortening of the vagina, which may be noticeable during intercourse.

*S*arah P had a hysterectomy at 65. She didn't really understand
what was involved in this operation and was afraid to ask her
doctor. She felt she was no longer a woman and couldn't get any
reassurance from her husband because he was worried that he might
somehow damage her if he had any sexual relationship with her.

  When she went for her check-up six weeks after the operation,
the surgeon asked her whether she had resumed intercourse. She
made it seem very natural and Sarah was able to ask all the
questions she had been so worried about, getting the reassurance she
needed.

It is usual for a couple to be able to restart intercourse about six
weeks after the operation, but love-making without penetration can
recommence much earlier, if both feel like it.

Prolapse operation

Prolapse is a bulging of the walls of the vagina and a loosening of
the uterine ligaments which, in mild cases can sometimes be treated by
the use of a small appliance called a pessary, but in severe cases can only
be cured by a quite extensive operation.

  It usually takes about six weeks for the tissues to heal, and there
may be soreness and discomfort for some time after that. However, sex
may be much more pleasurable when the healing is complete, as the
operation usually involves the vagina being made smaller, which can
give added sexual pleasure to both partners.

*S*pecific sexual problems

There are some problems which are more directly connected with
sexual performance. These problems can cause considerable anxiety
and distress, but much can be done to help.

Vaginal dryness and tightness

Many women find that after the menopause they produce less vaginal lubrication. This may be particularly noticeable when they become sexually aroused. The vagina remains dry, and this makes intercourse difficult and causes soreness and pain. It may be accompanied by an increasing tightness of the vagina and its entrance, which makes penetration extremely difficult.

This problem can be helped in two quite different ways. The first, and easiest, is to use cream or oil during intercourse. Sometimes the woman will apply this herself, but many couples find it enjoyable for the man gradually to insert the cream around the genitals and inside the vagina as part of foreplay. Vaseline will make things more difficult and painful, but a cream such as KY jelly, or any contraceptive cream or gel, will be very helpful. Some oils may be suitable, but they can be messy, and some scented skin oils may create soreness or a feeling of burning.

The lack of lubrication is due to the diminution of hormones that occurs after the menopause. Therefore the problem can be helped by some form of hormone replacement therapy. This may be given as tablets, by injection, by means of a plaster patch applied to the skin, by a cream containing hormones applied to the vagina or by a small pellet under the skin.

Hormone replacement is a widely used therapy that seems to have a positive effect on some diseases like osteoporosis and heart disease, but is not suitable for everyone.

The length of the treatment can vary but if a woman thinks it might help her, she should talk to her doctor or go to a well woman clinic, where she will find people willing to discuss the problems and offer practical help. (See *Seeking Help and Advice*.)

S ybil and Lionel L had always had a good sex life but gradually sex became painful for Sybil as her vagina was dry and seemed to be getting smaller. Lionel became increasingly worried about causing her pain but they felt they could not go to their young doctor for advice as they were certain he would laugh at them for wanting to enjoy this aspect of their married life. Some time later Sybil was troubled by a urinary infection and when the doctor examined her he told her that it looked as though she needed some hormones. He also asked her whether she was experiencing problems with intercourse. Sybil was surprised to find how easily she was able to talk to him, in spite of his youth. The hormonal treatment was very successful and she and Lionel were soon able once again to enjoy a very satisfactory sex life.

Vaginal bleeding and discharge

This may be the result of quite trivial causes. It can, however, signal something much more serious and therefore should be reported to the doctor as anything identified early is easier to treat.

Frigidity

This is a word that is often used as a term of abuse about women who appear not to respond to sexual advances. Coldness and the inability to be aroused are nearly always psychological and are often caused by previous painful sexual experiences or by a problem in the total relationship.

Many older women today were brought up to believe that marriage was the price men paid for sex, and sex the price that women paid for marriage.

Many men believed that the first intercourse for a woman was bound to be painful and therefore the sooner and quicker they managed it, the better it would be. The idea that women needed to be aroused with clitoral stimulation, and the opening to the vagina gradually stretched, was virtually unknown.

Until the 1950s most young women did not use tampons for sanitary protection. Virginity was precious and they were warned about the dire consequences of its loss. Some were even purposely frightened by their parents, who, with the best of motives, felt that this was the most effective way of ensuring that their daughters did not even contemplate allowing sexual intercourse before marriage.

At a time when birth control was still unreliable, sex was also threatening as the precursor of an unwanted pregnancy, and it was often believed that a woman could not become pregnant if she remained non-orgasmic.

All these factors added up to a powerful sexual turn-off and although some couples worked hard to try to reverse such early conditioning, others accepted women's inability to enjoy sex as inevitable.

Counselling and sensate focus therapy (see page 79) are both helpful in curing this condition. Very occasionally women are unable to be sexually aroused because of nerve damage, but this is relatively rare.

Erectile problems and impotence

Impotence is the inability to produce an erection. This may be total or partial and happen always or only occasionally.

It may be caused by an underlying physical disease such as diabetes or multiple sclerosis, or can be the result of drugs given to treat conditions such as high blood pressure, Parkinson's disease, or depression. Alcohol and nicotine can also affect potency.

Older men are likely to have less of the hormone testosterone circulating in their blood and this may cause some erectile problems, such as the penis never being very hard or erect, or even difficulties in achieving orgasm.

Psychological problems are an important cause of difficulties. Many men have been brought up to associate maleness and virility with the ability to perform sex satisfactorily. As a result, they tend to be very concerned about their own performance and may be upset to find that this varies with different partners. A new partner could be seen as a challenge or a threat or they may feel anger or resentment. Emotions such as these may be the sole reason for failure. This can also apply to a man who has remarried and finds that it takes quite a time to become fully potent with a new wife, after a period of abstinence.

Men can also, hardly surprisingly, become bored with repetitive, unexciting sex with an unresponsive partner and this, too, can in turn lead to diminishing desire. All of these may be helped by counselling and sensate focus therapy. There are also other more direct treatments for impotence including injections or penile implants.

POOR ERECTIONS

This problem can be helped by applying pressure at the base of the penis during intercourse. It can be done by hand or by the use of a specially designed penile ring. These rings can be bought at sex shops and are stocked by some chemists. If they are used they should not be worn for more than 30 minutes at a time. It is dangerous to try to apply pressure with rubber bands.

Special injections help to improve the strength of an erection. The exact dose will be determined by a doctor, and then the man will be shown how to do the injection for himself. This is quite painless and perfectly safe and will produce an erection in approximately 10 minutes that will last for about 30 minutes to two hours. This treatment can be used for poor erections due to a wide range of conditions such as diabetes or nervous diseases, or caused by psychological stress. It is not, however, always successful, and some men may find it unacceptable. Occasionally men may find that the erection does not subside when expected, but although uncomfortable, this is not dangerous.

PENILE IMPLANTS

There is a wide variety of different types of implants that will range from relatively simple, rigid supports to sophisticated pumps that can inflate a tube in the penis to make it erect. These implants will not increase a man's libido and desire for intercourse, even though his penis is erect. Having a stiff penis will, however, make sex play and intercourse possible. This may arouse desire, enable the man to enjoy intercourse, and sometimes lead to orgasm.

Premature ejaculation

Men will vary in their perception of whether they are ejaculating prematurely or not. Ejaculation before the penis enters the vagina or immediately afterwards would be considered premature, but as men vary in their ability to wait for orgasm, the length of time ejaculation is delayed after penetration will vary greatly.

However, it is possible to delay orgasm by light pressure between forefinger and thumb just behind the head of the erect penis. This can be applied by either partner and will diminish the feeling of urgency for ejaculation to occur. If the pressure is too firm the erection may subside completely.

Even a few feet is a long journey on a cold night.

6. *Improving your Sex Life*

'Grow old along with me.
The best is yet to be . . .'

Robert Browning

*L*ooking at anything as a problem is liable to turn it into something serious and daunting. When it comes to sexuality and personal relationships, there are likely to be difficulties for a range of reasons. Good sex is an art which requires practice and caring and for both partners a sensitivity to each other's needs.

It is always possible to improve love-making if both partners are willing to try. However, those who have been active sexually for a long time are not necessarily the most skillful. People who have only recently met can sometimes get a great deal of physical and emotional pleasure from love-making.

It must always be remembered that sex is something to be enjoyed by both partners. So if one finds it burdensome and unexciting or boring, tedious and a duty, that person is likely to magnify a difficulty into a problem, and the problem into an insurmountable barrier, so that sex eventually ceases altogether.

Not all problems can be solved, of course, but most can be broken down into their constituent parts. Once this is done, they can be discussed and examined and ways often found of improving the situation.

Talking about sex

The trouble for most of us is that we find it hard to talk about sex, even to our partners, and doubly difficult to approach someone such as a doctor, social worker or counsellor.

One part of the problem stems from the prevailing uncertainty as to whether older people should even be having sexual intercourse, let alone enjoying it. Another is created by the fact that most people who are now retired were brought up at a time when sex was not spoken about in terms of technique and performance. 'Was that alright for you?' is perhaps as much as most husbands are able to say, whereas 'What do you want us to do?' or 'Is there something that's not right?' are questions that are rarely asked. So, a certain number of people may get physical relief from sex while far fewer gain emotional satisfaction – let alone enjoy the spiritual dimension which can be part of a truly close relationship.

Boredom

Due to boredom, many older couples either slow down on the frequency of sexual intercourse or give it up entirely. Sometimes this is because the man is unimaginative in his love-making, believing that he must be the active partner who gets the satisfaction, and that the woman should be passive, gratefully receiving what pleasure might come her way.

On the other hand, some women have never enjoyed sex, nor expected to, and so have never responded to their husbands, however much they have tried to please. Those women who experience pain and discomfort will obviously not enjoy the experience and sometimes their partners, finding that they do not respond at all, become discouraged and stop trying.

Love-making, like anything else, has to be studied and practised if it is to produce the fulfilment that many couples enjoy, even after long years of marriage. For the same performance, at the same time on the same night in the same way will become boring for anyone and like any other boring experience is likely to be discontinued as soon as possible.

Changes over time

Sex can and should be fun: ranging from the new and unexpected to the known and the comfortable, from the exciting and tiring to the humdrum and everyday. Sometimes it will be exhausting, ending with orgasm for both partners, sometimes it may be tender, and almost non-genital, caressing and giving warmth and comfort. Sometimes one partner will be the more active, sometimes the other. Patterns of lovemaking should not be immutable and unchanging.

A couple who care for each other will normally try to respond to each other's needs. Sometimes only one partner will want sexual satisfaction and the other may be happy to be the giver. At other times one partner may masturbate, gaining pleasure and relief.

Sex may be fatiguing for older bodies. Sometimes orgasm is either difficult to achieve or else too tiring, except on relatively rare occasions, yet this does not mean that older couples are unable to enjoy a deep and satisfying love life.

Romance

Older people were brought up at a time when people often met formally and were used to a period of courtship before marriage. This has left them with a distinct advantage over today's young in that they have the ability to understand and enjoy romance.

This does not have to disappear over time as many happily married older couples know, and retirement can bring with it opportunities to reintroduce the romantic element which, for some, will have disappeared from their lives.

A memorable evening together can bring it back. Often the joy of preparing for sex, having a romantic supper and watching a film or bathing together may add hours of enjoyment to the pleasures that occur in bed. A short trip away from home requires a little research into that 'special offer' weekend or 'short break' holiday, but at such times other people create the atmosphere which can make it easier to discover something new and tender in a relationship. This can be delightful for people who are mobile, like to go away and can afford to do so.

Romantic evenings can also happen at home and if some preparation is needed, at last there is the time to do it. Special food, wine, lighting and music can all add an element of surprise, changing a humdrum evening into a magical one. We are all capable of finding that enchanting, particularly if it is a gift from the one person who understands what that special extra touch needs to be.

Single or double beds

A problem may be created by a move from a double bed into single beds. It may seem a rational thing to do when the marital double bed needs replacing. One partner may be more restless, or get up more often at night, snore, sleep badly, or want the light on. There may even be pressure from children, who don't expect their parents to be enjoying sex.

There are always seemingly good reasons for making the change and all are accompanied by the implicit assumption that sex is finished and that physical closeness is no longer wanted or needed. But this is palpably untrue. Many couples sleep better with the one they love close to them.

Once a couple have chosen to change to single beds they have to make a positive effort to make love. The comfort of closeness or of 'pillow talk' may be lost forever, and for most of us, once we are past the first fair flush of youth, making love in a single bed is neither a comfortable nor a safe pursuit, and falling asleep together in a single bed after love-making may be positively dangerous.

So it is that the couple in single beds find themselves making the journey across the room on fewer and fewer occasions.

Privacy

Problems may arise if a couple no longer have the privacy of their own home or if they are sharing accommodation and cannot lock their bedroom door. Sometimes children have a key to their parents' home and will visit without warning, not bothering to ring the bell. If it is considered necessary for there to be a keyholder, then it should be made quite clear that the key is only for use in an emergency. At all other times visitors should phone and say they are coming or else ring the bell and wait for an answer. Older people are no different from the young and if afraid of being disturbed or of making a noise, may be put off making love altogether. Privacy is an essential prerequisite to intercourse.

Retirement

Sexual problems frequently arise as a result of general marital disharmony, and many couples are shocked to find that a marriage that got along fairly well for thirty or forty years begins to come unstuck after retirement, often because expectations of life in retirement do not match up to the day-to-day reality.

Some women who do not have a job outside the home share their sense of impending doom with friends when they talk of their husband's retirement: They may say 'It will be strange having him around all day long', but what they mean is 'He will be interfering in everything I am trying to do' or 'I will spend the whole day making him meals and clearing up after him'.

Retirement is anticipated by most men not only as a time when they will no longer have to get up every morning and go to work, but also when they will have time to indulge in hobbies, be able to look after the garden and do all the other things they never previously had time to fit in. They are also inclined to imagine, rather naively, that their wives will enjoy having them share the household tasks. They do not realise that most wives have developed methods for getting chores done quickly, and don't want anyone telling them how they can work more efficiently or trying to reorganise their day.

Some wives would not mind an assistant who will do as he is told, but few men see themselves in that role, and many actually want to make wholesale changes in household routine. They also sometimes make tactless remarks about the time that their wives spend watching TV, chatting to neighbours or looking round the shops.

Another problem is that few men realise that their authority, both inside and outside the home, may depend on their ability to be a wage earner. The sudden affluence of time and shortage of money can create unexpected tensions and the man who no longer brings home the wage packet may no longer be able to call the tune.

Difficulties also occur as working women retire. They too may envisage retirement as an opportunity for relaxing and doing all the things that they had looked forward to for many years and may find the reality of adjustment just as difficult as men, particularly if they are also having to cope with a partner's problems.

Before retirement, many couples get on well because they spend relatively few hours together and because they have acquaintances and workmates with whom they can discuss the pleasures and irritations of daily life. When, as a result of retirement, those couples are suddenly thrown together for 24 hours of every day, they may find that they have few new things to talk about. They may bicker and criticize each other and within weeks or months yearn for any excuse to give them time apart.

It is not surprising that this increasing coldness and tetchiness with each other in the kitchen and living room, leads to coolness in the bedroom, and that resentment finds its way into love-making.

A woman who has had a row during the day with her husband may ignore his wish to make love at bedtime. 'I don't see why I should' she may think. 'Not until he's said he's sorry.'

'I don't see why I should' is something that many people think, but cannot say, because they are afraid of being ignored or ridiculed. In bed they do have the power, and frequently use it.

Equally, a husband may be upset when his wife rebuffs his offer of help in the house – ignoring his suggestions for a better working routine and then sulking when he goes down to the pub in the evening. 'I'm damned if I'm going to be nice to her in bed,' is his reaction.

Difficulties may also arise if partners are not able to adapt to changing sexual desires and always require their own individual needs to be met irrespective of the other's feelings. This innability to adapt may also show itself in other areas of life. A husband who has always had his lunch at a certain time during his working life may still want it at that time after retirement, while a wife may object to the idea of going out before all the housework is completed.

Most couples who get on fairly well do so because, over the years, they have achieved a way of living together which suits them both. They may not have been ecstatically happy, but they have managed well enough within the structure they have worked out for themselves. A large number of men and women do not particularly enjoy their work, so look forward to retirement as a time when everything will change for the better. Unfortunately the reality is often quite different.

There are, however, some people who get a great deal of job satisfaction and for them, retirement is a time of real loss. When they no longer have the stimulus of work or the status it provided, they become depressed and anxious and feel that they are no longer of use or value to anyone. This can have a profound effect on their own sense of personal worth and self-esteem and do serious harm to the way they relate to others, especially to those who are closest to them.

REAL NEEDS

Few couples talk to each other about real needs. At the beginning of marriage there are plenty of practical issues and problems to talk about, and once children arrive, there is usually little time to discuss personal feelings. In the brief time spent alone together, there are other things to talk about. Much of the conversation is focussed on the children's needs, rather than their own. A major change occurs when the children first leave home. By that time many couples have never spoken to each other about the things that really concern them.

Couples without children may be no better at communicating. Sometimes the childlessness has been involuntary and sexuality in earlier years was associated more with trying to become pregnant than with the goal of giving and receiving pleasure.

Those couples often carry a great sense of disappointment, which may reappear more strongly after retirement as they realise that they are getting old and will have no children to care for them when they become frail, and mourn the grandchildren they never had.

Single people may also carry similar pain. It is rarely helpful to remind them that there are couples with adult children who receive little support, love or caring from them, sometimes because the children live some distance away and sometimes because they do not seem to be very compassionate about their parents' needs.

It is therefore not surprising that many people reach retirement full of fears, hopes and anxieties that they are not able to express. Many feel that their partner ought to know and understand what they are feeling, without it being put into words.

Most of us tend to take our feelings for granted. We may not like them and want to change them, but most of us tend to imagine that others' responses to situations are identical to our own. However a moment's thought makes us realise that this is patently not true.

We are waiting in the checkout line at the supermarket and someone pushes his trolley in front of us in the queue. There are various reactions. We may feel angry and tell the offender to get to the back of the queue, or we may bottle it up and take it out on the next person we meet or kick the cat when we get home. Some of us may feel resentful or hurt. Others are resigned or feel victimised or blame the offender for being selfish or aggressive. We may even feel sorry for him for being such a rude, thoughtless person. The list of possibilities is endless. We certainly should not try and guess what anyone else in the queue is thinking. They may be feeling exactly the same as we do, but the chances are that their feelings will be very different.

The way that we respond to situations such as this is often based on our childhood experiences, and our responses depend more on the past than on the present. We each have our own favourite bad feeling and nearly always respond in the same way: angry or resentful; hurt or helpless, whatever the precipitating cause.

RETIREMENT COURSES

Some people now have the opportunity to attend retirement courses, either before or after leaving work. They can be very practical, with advice on finance, budgeting and earning extra cash as well as suggestions for taking up hobbies or acquiring new skills. The majority are very helpful, although occasionally some can be rather patronising as though retirement automatically topples everyone into extreme and decrepit old age.

Some of the best courses are specifically run for couples, with plenty of opportunity to talk about hopes and expectations, as well as fears and anxieties. Hearing others talk about their worries may give a couple their first opportunity to speak of things that have been at the back of their minds for some time. Sometimes offering advice to other people within the safety of a group may help an individual or a couple look at a problem that they had previously refused to face.

Similar problems to the ones that confronted couples when they first got married are likely to recur when they retire. The division of income, and whether each has separate money to spend or not; the allocation of time and decisions as to when each sees his or her own friends, are all likely to create friction unless there is a clear understanding of constraints and both partners agree on their new way of life.

Most retired couples slip into patterns of behaviour without sufficient thought as to whether they are either appropriate or meet the needs of them both. Sometimes they find that they lose contact with valued friends or that there are no longer opportunities to follow particular pastimes because one partner wants the other's undivided attention and resents sharing time with other people.

Such difficulties can emerge when couples find themselves spending unaccustomed long hours together. The realisation in advance that this is likely to happen helps to take the sting out of the situation when it does occur.

All these things need to be spoken about and retirement courses can provide a good opportunity to do so.

Remarriage

Many of us nowadays are married for a second or third time and we may have had bad marital experiences in the past which have left us incapable of being entirely open with our new partner. We may have a great deal of unfinished business: angers, hurts, humiliations, that we were unable to express either before or after the marriage break-up, and which we fear could be repeated. We may be afraid that scarcely healed wounds might be reopened and old pains reawakened. We may also feel that present discomforts could have been avoided if an idealised lost lover had still been with us.

There may be problems with children of a previous marriage. Most children, even as adults, are a bit like the curate's egg, 'good in parts'. If we are lucky the good outweighs the bad, but there are nearly always some ways in which our children do not match up to the expectations we have of them. For reasons of loyalty we are sometimes unable to share our feelings about this with our new partner, who may be more critical of them than we are ourselves, even if we know in our hearts that their criticisms are justified.

All these factors may affect the new partnership, sometimes leading to quarrels and lasting feelings of anger and resentment, which not only colour our emotional life but wreak havoc with our sexual relationship.

If fears and anxieties can be shared and couples can talk together about things that they want, some of the problems can be solved.

Seeking help

When problems are grave, they may reach a stage when sharing them with others makes them worse rather than better. Friends and relatives take sides and add fuel to the flames. At this stage the people intimately involved are likely to become increasingly depressed as they look to a future which seems to hold only argument, coolness and increasing anger. The resultant depression or psychosomatic problems may lead to a visit to the doctor for help.

General practititoners vary considerably in their sensitivity to the problems of older people. Sometimes their own expectation that retirement is bound to be a time of some strain and difficulty can make it hard for them to offer help and advice. Some doctors are very busy, and it seems to their patients that they do not have the time to listen to problems. Under these circumstances most people tell their doctor about their physical aches and pains, when they really want to talk about the pain of a relationship and their depression over a future which they see as unrelieved quarrelling.

Other doctors, however, are very willing to listen to problems and offer help, but even so this may require more time than they are able to give.

Counselling

Couples or individuals who need time and an opportunity to work through their problems may be helped by a counsellor. These people have been specially trained to listen to people in distress and help them to untangle the problem, to reach a solution or to come to terms with their situation. Counsellors will see couples together or separately. They will help with a marital problem even if only one partner is willing to consult them. People need time to say everything that they are feeling. They also need time to be able to sit quietly and listen to what their partner is saying.

The most important factors in the eventual successful outcome of any form of counselling are the individuals' ability to acknowledge that there really is a problem and their willingness to change. This can be quite daunting for older couples who may be reluctant to think about a new way of living and who may find themselves having to ask someone young enough to be their child or even their grandchild for help.

It may be even more difficult if the problems are sexual, for many older couples themselves wonder whether it is right for them to be having sexual feelings. They may be afraid of being laughed at if they seek advice or be fearful of being told 'What do you expect at your age' or 'You ought not to be having feelings like that at all – you must be abnormal'. This is unlikely to happen, but it is a risk that might have to be taken if help is really wanted.

Counsellors are sometimes attached to doctors' surgeries, or work at Relate (formerly the National Marriage Guidance Council). A nurse or social worker may be able to help and Citizens' Advice Bureaux (CABs) and Age Concern local groups will often be able to recommend a counsellor or suggest places where counselling services or other appropriate agencies are available. There are also sex counsellors who have particular skills in helping couples to overcome sexual problems.

Sensate focussing

This is the treatment pioneered by Masters and Johnson in the United States and sometimes known by their names. It is particularly suitable for couples who are having sexual difficulties and arousal problems, such as impotence and frigidity and the inability to enjoy sex. It concentrates on each partner giving and receiving pleasure rather than worrying about sexual intercourse and climax.

Doctors and therapists vary in their methods, but basically the treatment consists of three separate phases. During the first the couple are told to try to discover the non-genital sensation that each enjoys. They are taught to take it in turns to stroke each other's arms, face, legs and body for five or ten minutes at a time. Sometimes they are advised to use a lotion or cream to increase sensation. It is the responsibility of the receiving partner to tell the one who is doing the stroking what is enjoyable, whether a light touch or heavy pressure is more soothing or exciting, and for them both to explore the whole body, except the genitals, to find which areas are most sensitive to stimulation.

It is an important part of the treatment that each partner should tell the other what they like or dislike, and what turns them on. Most therapists will recommend that at this stage of treatment there should be no sexual intercourse, however much the couple desire it. The fact that they are both aroused, but not having to 'perform' may be important in reassuring them both and allow them to enjoy the sensations of their bodies.

Once both partners are happy about their responses to this phase, they will be allowed to move on to the second. This will always be preceded by the first phase of mutual non-genital pleasuring, and will progress to genital stimulation. Again the couple will be told to explore different sensations of touching, stroking, caressing, kissing and licking and to tell each other what is pleasurable. Most couples will find this extremely stimulating, but again they will probably be told not to attempt penetration.

Once they have mastered this phase they will be allowed to attempt the third, which includes phases one and two, but which may now go on to full intercourse and orgasm. This process may last several weeks, during which most therapists will wish to see the couple several times, to discuss their feelings and any problems or difficulties that they may be experiencing.

Sensate focussing is usually a very successful treatment because it gives a couple the opportunity to get to know each other and the things that each finds pleasurable. Many couples have previously failed to do this because they believed that the only goal of intercourse is orgasm.

The earlier stages of sensate focussing are particularly good for older couples, even if they are not experiencing severe problems, for they lengthen the time span of sexual enjoyment and require much less expenditure of energy. (See *Seeking Help and Advice.*)

Renewing Desire

A number of women probably feel, with some resentment and justification, that sex only takes place when the man feels like it, because that has been their experience. They may be very surprised to hear that it is not only acceptable, but often also appreciated, for a woman to be the prime mover, the arouser, the stimulator, awakening dormant sexual feelings and initiating love-making. It may seem trite to hand out the sort of advice that women's magazines usually give, but it would be foolish to pretend that their advice is only for the young.

A change of nightwear for either partner may do wonders. Bathing together can be exciting, particularly with pleasant smelling bath salts or talcum powder. Most people do not want to be embraced by anyone who is dirty or who smells unpleasant. On the other hand the odour of fresh sweat or of sexual arousal may be exciting to both men and women. Going to bed and making love during the day may be unusual but can be very enjoyable. It may be hard to change deeply entrenched habits but the results can be well worth the effort.

New positions

Many couples have only used one or two positions for intercourse throughout their married life, and although sexual acrobatics are probably inappropriate for those who are older, changes in positions can in themselves produce new sexual sensations.

The missionary position, in which the man lies on top of the woman, supporting his weight on his arms, may be tiring for the older man as well as being quite uncomfortable for the woman, if he is much heavier than she is. There is a range of positions in which the woman takes the superior position and lies or sits astride her partner. These have an added bonus, as both partners have their hands free to sexually stimulate themselves or their partner. Lying side by side with the man behind his wife may be a very suitable position for older couples as it is less tiring, and also provides an opportunity for maximum manual stimulation.

Perhaps one of the problems is that many couples regard sex as an entirely genital activity. Some men use their hands to stimulate their wives, but fewer wives think it is right or proper for them similarly to stimulate their husbands. Yet finding new ways of arousing sexual feelings can be as exciting for older people as it is for the young.

Enjoying sex

However adept individuals may think themselves as lovers, it is necessary to remember that love-making consists of two quite separate aspects.

The first is to be attuned to our partner's needs, to listen to what is being said or indicated by actions, and respond accordingly. Some people like kissing and caressing before any genital contact is made. Some enjoy a great deal of manual genital stimulation – indeed some women may only reach orgasm by stimulating the clitoris which is the small pea sized knob between the fleshy lips in front of the entrance to the vagina. Some women will want and need multiple orgasms to satisfy them.

Older men may be slower in their responses or they may want their partners to wear particular night clothes or use perfume in order to 'turn them on'. Some may fear that they will be unable to maintain an erection and reach orgasm, or make a fool of themselves; either partner may feel shy at exposing an ageing body to a new lover.

Any of these worries is likely to cause problems and it is probably helpful for a couple to try to share fears and anxieties. This may be very difficult for those who have never previously discussed their sexual needs or their sexual feelings, but being able to talk will not always be necessary.

The essence of good communication is listening and hearing what the other person is saying. Very often the message is not put into words but it is nearly always evident in actions and behaviour. Being sensitive to these and responding appropriately can help a relationship grow and become more satisfying for both partners without any words being spoken.

Many problems will disappear if each partner is able to be patient and caring towards the other, realising that a good sexual relationship may take time to develop.

The second aspect is to remember that we must all take and accept responsibility for our own sexual satisfaction. It is not enough for a woman to lie back and wait for a partner to satisfy her, nor for a man to complain that his partner is unresponsive.

It is our own responsibility to see that we manage to get the stimulation and satisfaction we need. Just because someone cares for us, this does not mean that they will automatically know what we want or where or when. No-one should be afraid, in love-making or in other areas of life, of telling their partner what they want and asking for what they need. If partners are expected to guess, it is not surprising that they sometimes guess wrong. Everyone must try to share feelings in anticipation of trust, otherwise they are unlikely to achieve the fulfilment they are looking for.

Masturbation

There have been times in the past when masturbation was considered to be sinful and likely to lead to grave disability and moral degeneration. Most people nowadays accept that it is not only harmless, but also enjoyable. It can help people to relax and relieve tension, and release the energy that might otherwise be used in trying to suppress sexual feelings. Everyone has some sexual needs and people who do not have a partner, and often those who do, may nevertheless find pleasure in stimulating themselves sexually.

Meeting our own needs

There was probably a puritan streak in the way most of us were brought up in the years between the two world wars, in which we were subtly led to believe that self-indulgence in any form was sin. This, of course, does not only apply to sex. It also applies to food, so we feel guilty about eating those extra chocolates or buying something special for ourselves. The truth, of course, is that we should have a sense of responsibility towards ourselves. We have a responsibility to go to the doctor when we are ill; but although the doctor will give advice or recommend treatment, it is our task to take charge of our bodies and make certain that they recover as quickly and completely as possible. Similarly, we must each take responsibility for making the most of all aspects of our lives, and this includes sex.

Sex games

Most people have sexual fantasies and although some undoubtedly are bizarre and only for the imagination, others can be happily shared as 'sex games', giving pleasure to both partners.

We have to try to put preconceived ideas out of our minds, and as long as we do not hurt or harm anyone else, we should not be afraid of trying new things.

Sex aids

Sex aids are another way of improving love-making. Until recently they were often considered to be unnatural, even 'kinky', but during the last twenty years they have become much more widely used by a large number of couples. Vibrators and dildos can give pleasure to both men and women, and can be of particular use to the older couple, as a mechanical aid can diminish the work needed to give each other maximum pleasure.

J oe and Mavis T lived in a small Midlands town. They had
always enjoyed sex and had tried to bring variety into their
love-making throughout their long married life. They had heard
about sex aids and discussed them together, but did not know how
much they would cost or where to get them. The only sex shop in
their town had one window painted black and another displaying
nothing but rather lurid underwear. Although they were prepared to
go in the shop when no-one they knew was around, they were afraid
of coming out and being seen.

Because of this they went to a neighbouring town and found
themselves wandering around the streets looking for a sex shop and
unable to ask anyone for directions. Fortunately they were able to
laugh at their predicament and realise that they needed to pluck up
enough courage to go into the local shop and purchase what they
wanted. They were rather surprised to find that the woman in the
shop was very helpful.

Sex aids are also a help to people who are on their own and to those
for whom manual stimulation may be tiring or unsatisfactory. They
may be no substitute for a lover but can provide a great deal of physical
pleasure. But the embarrassment many people feel about having them
at home can take away any pleasure and relief of tension they might
bring.

D oris M an elderly widow confided that she was very worried
about what her niece, who was her next of kin, might think
when she came to clear up her flat and dispose of all her belongings
after her death, as she was bound to do eventually. It would
undoubtedly have helped her if she had been able to speak frankly
to her niece.

Both vibrators and dildos are shaped like an erect penis and some
have small attachments which can also be bought separately, for clitoral
stimulation. Vibrators and dildos cost approximately between £10 and

£30. There are also padded condoms that can be worn by men to increase the size of the penis and this may improve vaginal stimulation.

Artificial vaginas range from small tubes with or without a vibrator, to full sized blow-up dolls. The smaller appliances cost about £15 to £30 and full sized dolls about £300 to £500. There is also an intermediate range for about £100.

Some sex aids run off batteries and some on mains electricity. The latter may not always be convenient but tend to be more reliable, as batteries wear out.

Sex shops sell a wide range of products designed to produce many types of stimulation. Some people wanting a sex aid may prefer to obtain a catalogue to look at in the privacy of their own homes. It may take some time to decide and many people may feel uncomfortable spending time in a sex shop trying to make up their mind.

Catalogues are available from shops or can be sent by post. There is usually a charge for these and as they are designed to be titillating, they may cause embarrassment or even offence.

Most catalogues include a wide range of tablets and creams that promise better sex. Lubricants can do a lot to increase pleasure but products that claim that they can produce a harder erection are rarely of value, although the emotional stimulation of using them may produce some improvement.

Watching explicit movies together may also be stimulating and arouse sexual feelings. Such films, which can be obtained from most video shops under the section 'Adult Movies', may range from overt shots of couples enjoying sex to a variety of partnerships and positions.

Oral sex

Oral sex, the stimulation of genitalia with the tongue and lips, is a pleasure that some couples might like to try, but they are afraid of broaching the subject. It is not something that everyone will want to experiment with, but many couples have heard about it. Some wonder if it is as enjoyable as it is supposed to be. Others, because sex and excretory organs are close together and so inextricably linked in people's minds, do not fancy it at all. They might find it more acceptable if they were certain that their partner's body was clean and sweet smelling. There are some people who consider oral sex a perversion that should not even be thought about, let alone tried. Others want to experiment and might be helped by the knowledge that to do so is not abnormal. Anyone, regardless of age, should feel free to try anything that they and their partners are happy about and with which they feel comfortable and at ease, provided that it does not conflict with their own overriding principles or beliefs.

'*Is that what the doctor meant?*'

7. *Being Alone*

'I am spending delightful afternoons in my garden, watching everything living around me. As I grow older, I feel everything departing, and I love everything with more passion.'

Emile Zola

*T*ogetherness and sharing are so often sold by the media as being the ideal that it is tempting to assume, quite wrongly, that everyone wants to live with family, friends or a partner.

It is necessary to differentiate between being alone and being lonely. Many of us are perfectly content with our own company. We wish to live alone and are happy to find companionship outside the home, making friends and inviting them to visit for relatively brief periods. We enjoy the freedom that this independence brings. On the other hand there are many others among us who feel desperately lonely in spite of physically living with someone else.

Problems arise for anyone who hates being alone, but has to tolerate it, because there is no choice. It is probably particularly difficult for those of us who lose a partner to adapt to being single again, with all the trauma that this sometimes involves.

The surviving partner

Adjusting to the loss of a partner is usually a long and difficult process. For most widows and widowers, the loss of a companion and friend and the loneliness of no longer being a couple are difficult to bear. There are also many practical problems that have to be sorted out for a survivor who is unused to coping with paying bills or doing DIY, or who has never done any cooking other than making a cup of tea. Yet these pale into insignificance when compared with the loss of someone to chat to, someone who can share the major problems and joys as well as the inconsequential events of everyday life.

The interminable nights struggling for elusive sleep and the long dark evenings of loneliness may never become bearable. Family, friends and neighbours are usually kind, but their support tends to disappear as time goes on and there is often the feeling, even if unexpressed, that it is about time to start 'pulling yourself together and feeling better'. Most people take years to adapt to being on their own after years of partnership. Others never succeed in being anything other than half of a couple that no longer exists.

The pain of this overwhelming loss is often made worse, because the surviving partner quite unexpectedly finds that he or she still has sexual feelings that demand satisfaction. Some of the need may be for touching, comfort and caring, but some people still have strong physical sexual desires.

These create extra confusion for those for whom it is already a struggle to find emotional stability, and the lack of open discussion arouses fears that no-one else has such feelings or desires. The conspiracy of silence that society imposes on this topic often prevents widows and widowers seeking appropriate advice and reassurance.

All these problems are also experienced by the surviving partner of a homosexual or lesbian relationship, with the added difficulty in some cases of having to keep the sense of bereavement secret and therefore being unable to share the grief with others.

Because the sexual needs of older people are ignored or rarely talked about, many find it difficult to turn to anyone for help, fearing that they will be laughed at or else rejected for having such 'improper' feelings at a time of loss. This is understandable, because all too often well-meaning individuals make value judgements about other people's behaviour and speculate quite incorrectly about their feelings, very often misinterpreting a widow or widower's renewed social activity as lack of feeling for a recently deceased partner.

Reacting to stress

We react to stress in very different ways. Most of us have little control over our feelings, although we do try to keep our actions within acceptable limits. Some people have a continual need for food when they are miserable, while others find that the mere thought of food at times of stress makes them feel ill. Some are thrown into a fever of activity when they become anxious, talking endlessly to anyone available; while others want to do nothing but sit in gloomy silence. Some people have to visit the lavatory every few minutes when they get nervous, others get rashes or headaches when they worry. All these are normal responses that occur as the body reacts unconsciously to stressful circumstances.

Our sexual feelings are, similarly, not totally under our own control, but this does not mean that people who have lost their partners necessarily behave in a sexually unacceptable fashion. They may, however, find themselves becoming sexually aroused, and be uncertain as to whether they should try to satisfy these feelings or attempt to suppress them.

Many feel guilty at the thought of self-stimulation, but learning to accept it as being as normal as anything else that was formerly done together, but now has to be done alone, may help those without a partner.

There are lots of other things like eating, going for walks and shopping, that single people have to do by themselves. We are fortunately well past the days when widows were expected to wear black for the rest of their lives and have no pleasures other than those that were brought to them by the visits of children and grandchildren or other family members. Sexual pleasure is just one more thing that nowadays those who are alone have to find for themselves.

Divorce and separation

The situation for those who are divorced or separated is, in many ways, similar to those whose partner has died. Even after an unhappy marriage, the divorced and separated often experience great loneliness and isolation, and the feelings of deserted wives and husbands, whose partners have found someone new, can be very similar to those of the widowed.

Unfortunately, society rarely has much sympathy or compassion for people whose marriages have broken up. Perhaps there is often an underlying suspicion that 'they brought it on themselves'; but whatever the cause, little effort is made to understand the very real pain felt by this group of people and to help them meet their most ordinary everyday needs. It is not surprising that they may also be too embarrassed to seek advice and help when they find they still have sexual feelings and needs.

Singles

Among single people are those who have chosen to remain celibate and are happy that way and others who have had celibacy forced upon them, having never met anyone with whom they wished to share their lives and their bodies. There are also a large number of older single people, who have had good or bad sexual experiences with a partner or partners at some stage in their lives.

New friendships

So in talking about people on their own we are in fact referring to a large and varied group. Many are content just as they are. Others are looking only for friendship and companionship. There are those who are seeking a permanent relationship, while some would like the sharing to include sexual pleasuring but may be afraid of the reaction of family and friends.

Another real problem is the social expectation that everyone should have a partner. Couples invite other couples to their homes and single people are left out. A widow may find it particularly hurtful to be abruptly dropped by erstwhile friends on the death of her husband, and only invited to morning coffee or afternoon tea with other women. Dinner invitations tend to be for pairs, and partner-less people are not invited, except to make up numbers or to be introduced to a prospective new partner.

There is sometimes, too, an almost superstitious fear of widows among some women who, because they may not be very happily married or feel insecure, are scared of losing their husband to someone else – a sort of marital musical chairs with some of the contestants being expected to give up their seats. Many widows find themselves angry and embarrassed to be offered sexual favours by the husbands of friends as if they were being granted social services.

Trying new things

There is no reason why older people without a partner have to conform to the standards and expectations of others. Those of us who are single have fewer responsibilities for others and more responsibility to meet our own needs whenever possible. We are free to eat our breakfast at mid-day or have kippers at midnight. If we want to learn Russian, lampshade-making or plumbing or to take a course at the Open University, we should not be afraid to have a go. Similarly, if we want to enjoy a sexual relationship, and fully understand the nature of the commitment, then we should be prepared to take a chance. It might not be anything very great, but on the other hand it might prove very satisfying and enjoyable, cementing and deepening an already established friendship.

Cynthia L retired from a good job in local government. She had worked very long hours and never married but had enjoyed two very long term love affairs. When she retired she felt very lonely and missed the stimulus and companionship of the people at work. After a while she joined an art class and found that she had an untapped talent. This gave her immense pleasure, bringing her into contact with a new range of people whom she found extremely interesting and who shared her love of the history of art. Eventually a loving relationship developed between Cynthia and another member of the art class who was a widower living locally but whom she had never previously met.

Under the clock.

8. *Finding a New Partner*

'I look upon every day to be lost in which I do not make a new acquaintance.'

Samuel Johnson

*T*here are some very definite advantages in having a partner. At the most basic level it is good to have someone to talk to and share the joys and pleasures, the annoyances and the frustrations that are part of everyday life. It is pleasant when someone is available to share the unplanned walk or visit to the cinema. For most people, however, the rewards of a loving relationship extend to a much deeper level.

The problem for most of us is how to find this other person with whom we are going to share our life. Will we bump into Mr or Ms Right while out shopping or waiting for the bus, or is it necessary to be more active in finding a new partner? Perhaps we have to be more rational than when we were younger and hoped that falling in love would be an answer to all our dreams.

By the time the later part of life is reached, we should each have a fairly good idea of the sort of partner we are looking for. Lady Diana Cooper was reputed to have said, when her name was coupled with that of a man soon to be 100 years old: 'My dear, at my age you will realise that what you need is a maturer man!'

For most of us it would be realistic to think of looking for someone from a similar sort of background with interests we share. There are difficulties, however, especially for women, in finding such a partner, partly because the older people get, the more women there are relative to men.

For many people, however, the real problem is the lack of opportunity for meeting new partners. We may see interesting looking people around but find it difficult to start up a conversation.

Being adventurous and taking risks are probably not easy for anyone. Most of us are shy and do not easily talk to strangers. We may be afraid of being misunderstood. However people who are prepared to make the first overture may be surprised at how often they meet people they like.

Men and women may have different aims in seeking a new partner for although both are looking for companionship and friendship, there may be subtle differences in their social and emotional needs.

Single men

The situation of many older men on their own is often a mixture of power and fear. Almost everywhere they go they will find themselves outnumbered by women. This numerical imbalance may be a double edged sword, however. Many men admit to a fear of being 'gobbled up' by women who want a partner or a husband more as a sign of success than as someone to be loved for himself.

If a man goes to a club he might find himself surrounded by women, a large number of them looking for a partner, companion or friend, and therefore eager to appear to him in the best light.

A man alone can, if he is active, have a very easy life while women friends feed and cosset him, but may have problems in disentangling their motives. On the other hand, some men are, not unnaturally, looking for someone who will look after them and their home and cook, shop, wash and iron for them.

Single women

Many women are eager to find someone to marry and call their own, as well as seeking companionship and friendship. Being in a permanent relationship can confer upon a woman a subtle status. Those who have succeeded in this apparently competitive field are often regarded as more able or more attractive, or even better people than those who have not.

Making friends

A considerable number of friendships result from work contacts and from getting to know other people through children's friends. Even when these contacts are maintained, most older people still find that their world becomes smaller, although they may continue to see some friends and acquaintances. On the whole opportunities to make new friends seem few and far between.

Many new relationships can and do start from regular meetings at lunch clubs or special interest groups.

J osef H and Rosa G had got to know each other through meeting regularly at a local gardening club. Their meetings progressed to going to the cinema together once a week on a Wednesday afternoon. As they got closer, Josef fell into the habit of going back to Rosa's flat for tea. As the days got shorter she asked him if he would like to stay the night, which then became a regular event.

Some friendships, however, which might have developed further do not for a variety of reasons. There may be a fear of exploitation, or even a lack of opportunity because children or neighbours have a spare key to the home. Very often a couple do not even attempt to explore their sexual potential because they wonder 'if it is right' or 'what the family would say if they knew'.

Another fear that may lurk at the back of people's minds is what would happen if one of them had a heart attack and how would it be explained if they were found in bed with someone to whom they were not married. These may be very real obstacles and it would certainly be wrong for people to do something against their moral code or all they believed to be right.

A large number of older people are very content to enjoy friendships without them developing into any form of sexual relationship.

Dating agencies and marriage bureaux

Social clubs are the places where some single people go to try and make friends and perhaps find a new partner. However, many dislike the atmosphere or may even be afraid of the overt feeling of competition that is somehow generated and may therefore prefer to go to an agency.

There are many such agencies in existence and they vary in their efficiency and in their aims. Some set out to provide prospective husbands and wives; others only to find casual or semi-casual acquaintances for friendship, shared interests and companionship.

Clients also vary in their expectations, and it is important that, from the beginning, all applicants try to find out as far as possible what the people they meet want from a relationship. Those who approach each encounter with 'stars in their eyes' are likely to be disappointed, for although most clients want to be open and honest, there are some who are in it for what they can get and will present themselves in a false light.

It is important for older people to remember for themselves all the good advice that they would and do give to grandchildren or nieces and nephews going out on a date, for older people face almost exactly the same pitfalls in choosing a new partner as those 30 or 40 years younger.

There are a large number of options, and we are all different people wanting different things. Some want a long term relationship and someone to live with or marry. Others want to retain their independence and only seek companionship and a friend to see a few times a week. For some, sex may be an important part of the relationship, while for others, it may be unimportant or even totally unwanted. It is therefore necessary for each of us to try to work out for ourselves not only what we want, but also what we do not want – otherwise disappointment is likely to follow.

Trying to make a partner change

It is never wise to get married in the hope that someone will change or can be changed. While some people do, the changes that happen are rarely the ones we strive for. We have to try and be as realistic as possible and get to know the true person under the superimposed image we have created.

*F*rank C, aged 70, wanted someone to replace his cherished wife, who had died the previous year. She had done everything for him, looked after the house and done the cooking. Frank had been a good husband, father and provider.

Then he met Dora who seemed just like his late wife. She was a good cook and an interesting companion, who attended several day classes and enjoyed going for walks, reading and the theatre.

When they got married he was surprised that Dora wanted to continue her day classes and expected Frank to help with the housework. They both had a commitment to make this marriage work and spoke to a counsellor from Relate (formerly the Marriage Guidance Council), who helped them build a relationship that took account of each other's needs.

Sometimes as we get older we tend to slip into commitments very quickly. We may be afraid that there are few years left to enjoy each other's company or that someone else will come along and capture our prospective partner. But it is particularly important for us to be quite certain that we are embarking on the right course, as we may have more to lose than younger people if we take risks.

However attractive a proposition might appear to be, it is necessary to give plenty of thought and as much time as possible to it, before making any decision that involves a major change in lifestyle. This is particularly true when it could mean giving up a home or inviting someone else to share it. Such decisions are likely to be irreversible. It may be relatively easy to get a divorce if a marriage goes wrong, but difficult to find anywhere else to live if sharing accommodation does not work out.

Marriage is for many of us the only acceptable way to live together; it also demonstrates a commitment of each to the other. But some are reluctant to take this step and must therefore do what they feel is right for them.

As we get older, many of us become wary of making major changes in our lives for we realise that once we do it is often difficult to change back.

This is particularly true for retired people who are actively involved in a range of interests, and realise that they may have to make a choice between the benefits of a new relationship and the loss of hard-earned independence. Everything in life has a price and it is for each of us to work out for ourselves what we are being asked to pay, whether what we are being offered is worth the price and whether we are willing to pay it.

*M*argaret G had been widowed for ten years and had made a full life for herself since her retirement. She worked as an adviser on a part-time basis, was a Samaritan volunteer, and also a member of the management committee of an organisation caring for disabled people.

She became increasingly friendly with Ian K, who had been widowed three years earlier and whom she had known through work for more than 15 years. He was also a Samaritan volunteer. They got on extremely well in all aspects of their relationship and Ian began to try to persuade Margaret to marry him or at least to live together.

Margaret would have liked to do this but it had taken her many years to find self-fulfilment and she was reluctant to give up any of her interests or her independence. She was also afraid that she might find herself running a home for Ian and even having to care for him if he ever became frail.

She realised that she might be the one to become frail one day and risk having no-one to look after her then. This she felt was a risk that had to be taken, for if she did give up her interests and married Ian and then subsequently changed her mind, it might be impossible for her to revert to her previous lifestyle.

Understanding our needs

Most people get married because they are attracted by their partner's good qualities or because they think that the 'chemistry' is right. Both of these are fine, but it is realistically much more important to identify a prospective partner's less attractive and desirable characteristics and decide whether these can be lived with and are tolerable, or totally impossible.

We are all, fortunately, different in what we want and what we are able to tolerate, but most of us can live with kindness, empathy, generosity, tenderness and emotional stability. What we each have to decide is whether we can put up with the untidiness or the forgetfulness, the obsessional tidiness, the procrastination or the meanness, the untruthfulness or laziness that may also be part of another person's make-up. Whether we are young or old we are all the normal human mixture of good and bad. None of us is a saint and very few are out-and-out sinners. There are things that we each can put up with and things that drive us crazy. By the time we are in our later years we should at least have made an effort to identify what we want or do not want in a new partner, even if it is not possible to look at ourselves totally objectively.

On the other hand, it is equally important to be realistic about what we are likely to be able to achieve, realising that we may have to settle for less than we really wanted. Women are unlikely to find that dream millionaire who is strong, amorous, handsome and caring, only wanting to love and to give. Equally, men are unlikely to find Marilyn Monroe look-alikes willing to cook, clean, care for and devote all their lives to them.

In settling for something less than ideal, the important thing is to know exactly what we have settled for. However kind and mature two people may be as individuals, once they become a couple, there is always the need for radical adjustment as they adapt to thinking about the needs of another, rather than the self-interest that may have been the motivating force for years when they were on their own.

Children's feelings

When forming new relationships, older people may have to consider the feelings of children or grandchildren of a previous marriage, or even nieces and nephews.

Some children feel upset at the idea of a step-parent taking the place of a much loved mother or father. They may feel hurt at the thought of personal belongings or family heirlooms being used by someone else. They may decide that their surviving parent should stay unmarried and unattached or may quite arbitrarily choose the time they think is appropriate to elapse after a death before anyone else joins the family. They may be afraid that a new partner will take away an inheritance, however big or small that may be, or may be anxious that the family home in which they previously felt at ease and comfortable, could become strange and unwelcoming.

These fears and anxieties may be understandable – based on the reality of the situation, or they may be quite irrational – the result of pure fantasy. However, it is unwise to brush them aside and pretend that they do not exist. Unless they can be examined and discussed, they may create difficulties between parents and children that can destroy the new relationship and the established family one, too, as parents find themselves torn between conflicting loyalties.

Many children tend to stereotype their mothers and fathers without attempting to examine the real needs of a surviving parent. This is not altogether surprising, for the way we see our parents is the result of what we have experienced over many years and often relates to our own character and needs, rather than the real character and needs of our mother or father.

Children often feel very responsible for an elderly surviving parent, even if in truth they do little more than ensure that the parent is warm, well fed and not ill. Their attitude may be similar to the way they regard their own children, preferring their surviving parent or child to be dependent and compliant, rather than independent and thus an unknown risk factor.

It is unwise to antagonise children unnecessarily, but it is equally unwise for parents to live their lives to fit their children's convenience and expectations.

On the other hand there are many children who are supportive and welcome a parent's new partner, going out of their way to ensure that he or she is made to feel a full member of the family.

SAFEGUARDING INTERESTS

It may help children and parents to agree on a formal document spelling out the respective rights of both parties and the children of previous marriages.

It is sometimes embarrassing to talk about wills, but it may be more straightforward for everyone to know their exact legal position

8080

rather than harbouring suspicions and prejudices. New partners too may feel more secure knowing that step-children will not turn them out of their home if their partner should predecease them. Children, similarly, will be more comfortable in their relationship with a step-parent if they know that the family home will revert to them on the step-parent's death, rather than passing on to that step-parent's own children.

Past experiences

Any new partnership is likely to be affected by the nature of each individual's past experiences, whether a previous relationship has been good or bad, and whether it has been long lasting or fairly short lived.

Those who have been widowed after a long and successful marriage may idealise the past and compare any new partner unfavourably with the one who has died. On the other hand, success tends to breed success and those who have been in a mutually satisfying long term relationship may be more able and willing to identify the needs of others and forge an equally happy marriage, even though it may be very different from the previous one.

Those who have been divorced may be disillusioned and bitter, and unable to trust a new partner completely. On the other hand they may have gained insight into the reason why things went wrong for them in the past and understand much more about their own shortcomings and their previous difficulties. With this knowledge they will be able to be more positive in the new marriage.

Jean J had never enjoyed sex during her long marriage because her late husband had been totally uncaring and concerned only with his own satisfaction. She was very worried when at the age of 70 Ralph B, whom she had known for six months and whom she liked very much, asked her to marry him. He seemed quite different from her first husband and she thought that her strong sexual feelings were shared by him. However she was very scared and thought history might repeat itself. Luckily she was able to discuss this quite frankly with Ralph and after talking this through in depth with him, she was confident enough to get married and things turned out very well for them both.

Some people may have had one or two long relationships. Others may have had several that have been fairly ephemeral.

Some who contract new partnerships may never have been married before. They may have lived alone or with an elderly parent and adapting to living within a partnership may require a lot of learning and understanding. No one experience is more likely than another to produce success.

Working at a relationship

If a partnership is to blossom and begin to meet the needs of both people involved, it is necessary for each to work hard at the relationship and try to understand the other's needs. Both partners must be willing to look at their own behaviour and responses. Are they always appropriate to the present, or are they learned reflexes that really relate to things that happened years ago with other people?

The sexual relationship will also require thought and understanding as well as sensitivity to another's needs. We all vary in our sexual responses and what we want and enjoy. The needs of the new partner may be quite different from those of a previous partner.

The past in perspective

It is important for anyone starting a new partnership to decide how much of the past should be shared. Some people will be reluctant to tell too much of the private intimacies that went on in the past between husband and wife and may feel disloyal to a previous partner in saying too much. Others may want to tell all. Either course could prove to be embarrassing or upsetting, so it is perhaps necessary for all older couples to set boundaries for themselves and discuss at an early stage of the relationship what is to be shared and what is to remain private.

When we talk about sexual experience and a new partner we tend to think of love between a man and a woman, but it might also mean the loving of two people of the same sex. If two adults can find companionship, enjoy each other's bodies and give pleasure to the other as well as finding pleasure for themselves, this can be as deeply satisfying and rewarding a relationship as that between a man and a woman.

It is yet another area in which we each have to make our own choices.

There's more to it than cycling.

9. *Living*

'Old age has its pleasures which though
different, are no less than the pleasures
of youth.'

W Somerset Maugham

*F*or many of us retirement will extend from 20 to 30 years. So it is worth ensuring that we can enjoy life to the full, sharing in shaping our community, enjoying the facilities around us and contributing to the wider society.

*K*eeping in Good Shape

We can do a lot to prevent disease and disability in later life by taking sensible care of ourselves physically and emotionally while we are still relatively fit.

A certain amount of real ageing does take place, but it need not destroy our capacity to enjoy life. Total body transplants are unlikely to become widely available within the next few years, so we may as well keep the one we have in as good a trim as possible.

Time to share

One of the consolations of ageing is that many people's personality actually seems to improve markedly as they get older. They become more confident in their approach and young children are often impressed by their grandparents' capacity to listen to them and to share their enthusiasm. This is often because older people have time to spare and are happy to spend it with the younger members of the family, which is particularly important when so many parents are preoccupied with busy work schedules outside the home. If older people are valued and loved it usually has more to do with the attractiveness of their personality than with the ephemeral nature of good looks. This is not to suggest that appearance is unimportant. Keeping well groomed and making the best of oneself are prerequisites to feeling good at any age.

Keeping active

Unfortunately, it often happens that people do start to neglect their appearance and grooming as they get old. One extremely active elderly lady said that the important thing was always to put on outdoor shoes. 'The day people only wear slippers,' she said, 'was the start of a "slippery slope" of not bothering. It then becomes too much of an effort to do your hair and to wash and eventually you become housebound.' She was probably right. Everyone needs to keep active and to get up in the morning and go out if at all possible. If walking or even moving around the house is to be comfortable, feet should be kept in good order through regular chiropody appointments.

Exercise

Regular daily walking is good for everyone and swimming is an ideal activity, of benefit to the whole body. It is never too late to begin some toning up exercises though these should be tailored to individual needs.

Keep-fit TV slots and video tapes are useful for those who don't mind exercising alone but for most of us it is far easier to keep going within the companionship of a group. Local Age Concern groups or old people's welfare/senior citizens' clubs may run keep-fit classes or they may be able to advise on where to go. People who have not exercised recently should check their state of health with their doctor before embarking on anything strenuous.

Healthy eating

We should try to eat sensibly, avoiding too much salt and animal fats. We all need plenty of fruit and vegetables and an adequate amount of high bulk foods such as wholemeal bread and hi-bran cereals, though the old saying that a little of what you fancy does you good is nearly always right. Smoking, dangerous at all ages, should be stopped if possible, and alcohol consumption cut down, although a drink late at night can be beneficial, help relaxation at the end of the day and induce sleep.

Obesity

Obesity is a problem for many older people. Many comfort themselves when they are depressed and miserable by eating, remembering childhood days when a chocolate or food was offered as solace, telling themselves that wearing easy-fitting, less fashionable clothes will help to hide the bulges. Once that has happened, though, it becomes more and more difficult to call a halt to weight gain, and people tend to eat yet another chocolate or doughnut, trying to console themselves by saying 'it doesn't matter at my age'.

The problem is that it does matter. Thinness is not something to hanker after, but fatness should be avoided whenever possible. Overweight people are more prone to heart disease, high blood pressure and arthritis than thinner people, and being overweight can be an extra danger factor in the event of surgery. Fat people, too, are more likely to get breathless, or to get sore places where the rolls of fat rub together.

Being two stone overweight is like walking around perpetually attached to two heavy shopping baskets. No wonder people are healthier, get less tired and have more energy, if they stay near the normal weight for their height.

There is another problem in being overweight, and that has to do with body image. Fat people begin to be ashamed of their bodies and reluctant to let anyone, even their partner, see them without clothes. This may not matter for those who have been married for a long time, but can be very embarrassing for those starting a relationship – quite apart from which it may put off their new partner.

It is not easy, particularly for those people whose only pleasure is eating, to lose weight, but it is important to try to keep body size under control by sensible and balanced eating. This can sometimes be easier for a couple than for a single person as two people are able to give each other moral support and hide those tempting cakes and chocolates.

If, however, obesity is a problem during intercourse the heavier partner should adopt the less active role and should not attempt to lie on the slighter partner. Neither suffocation nor flattening add to sexual pleasure for most people.

General health

It is essential for older people to have a regular annual check-up with their doctor. For women this should include gynaecological tests and breast examinations. Early detection of cancer is imperative and is just as necessary in later life as when young. If a doctor does not provide this service, check with the local community health council to find out where a local health clinic is operating. Some doctors now offer 'well older women's' and 'well older men's' clinics which encourage people to take care of themselves, to keep fit and well and prevent disease.

Hearing

Hearing difficulties affect one in three elderly people. It is one of the most isolating conditions and yet, surprisingly, a great many people are reluctant to admit they can no longer hear very well, and do not seek help. Hearing aids can be very difficult to use, because all sounds get magnified, and it takes time to differentiate speech from the heightened background noise. It is essential to persevere with their use, because many hearing people often have little patience with deafness and surprisingly little sympathy for the problems it brings. A hearing aid can quite literally transform a deaf person's life.

Sight

Regular eyesight tests are important and should never be neglected. Serious conditions, such as diabetes or hardening of the arteries, which need medical attention, can often be identified through routine checks. Glaucoma and other serious eye diseases which can lead to blindness may be avoided through regular examinations conducted by a qualified practitioner.

Sleep

Sleep patterns change with age. Most of us need more frequent rest but less long, deep sleep and therefore should, if tired, take regular rest periods during the day, preferably lying down in bed.

Many people sleep less soundly during the night and have to adjust to being awake for long periods. It can be helpful to think of such hours as additional time for reading, listening to the radio, watching TV or writing letters, rather than as time which must be devoted to trying to sleep at all costs. Sleeping tablets may help, but often have side effects and can make anyone who takes them feel 'under par' during the following day.

Teeth

Regular visits to the dentist are essential. The mistaken belief that once a person has dentures, there is nothing more for the dentist to do, creates much unhappiness and discomfort. The shape of the mouth changes throughout life, particularly in old age, and this causes dentures to fit badly, which can not only be painful when eating, but embarrassing. As a result, some elderly people stop going out and eating with others. This is sad because much could be done to make their mouths comfortable and to improve their appearance at the same time. Dentists can also detect early signs of serious disease.

Social life

Having friends and keeping in contact with them are important at all stages of life. As we get older some close friends may die. They are impossible to replace but we have to make an effort to make new friendships to avoid becoming isolated. This is never easy, but it becomes more difficult with increasing age. It is possible to broaden our circle of acquaintances by joining with groups of people who share a common interest. This might be dancing, music or local history, gardening, photography or many other activities. There are also local bird-watching and rambling clubs, and numerous opportunities for volunteering, through which new friendships can be made.

Local Age Concern groups usually run lunch clubs, 'pop-ins' or day centres, with a range of different activities to choose from and they

always need more volunteers to help run them. There are usually
opportunities to play bingo or bridge in most areas. Leisure centres are
now beginning to offer various activities scheduled at times convenient
for older people, while other centres cater specifically for people from
different cultural and ethnic backgrounds.

Local further and higher education courses are increasingly
welcoming older adults and people of all ages without preliminary
qualifications. The University of the Third Age is an interesting option
in some areas and is designed specifically for older people. Special
interest holidays can also be a good way of meeting people and making
new friends.

*M*oving Home

The decision to leave the home in which we may have lived for a
large proportion of our lives is a very great emotional upheaval. Many of
us will have spent most of our married life and brought up our children
there. It will be full of memories and every room evokes the past.

A move is generally considered to be one of the most emotionally
disturbing things that we go through, and this applies whether we move
from choice, after careful thought and planning, or from necessity
following a crisis such as the death of a spouse or a deterioration in our
general health. Either of these may be upsetting in themselves and
fraught with anxiety.

It is sometimes hard for younger people to understand just how
important familiarity is in older people's lives and how difficult it is to
adapt and feel really at home in new accommodation. Even when the
move has been made in a spirit of optimism and has been well thought
through and planned in advance, it can lead to much unhappiness, at
least initially.

As we age it is of the utmost importance that any decision to move
is our own and not a response to what other people feel is best for us.

Adult children, with the best of motives, may attempt to influence their parents at a time when they are least able to withstand such well meaning pressure.

Moving on retirement

Some couples decide that on retirement they will leave their present home and move some distance away, perhaps to the seaside or the country, exchanging the family home where their children grew up for something smaller and easier to run.

It is very important to consider what is likely to happen when two people are thrown together for 24 hours of each day without the support of close family and friends and, even more important, what life will be like for the survivor, when one partner dies. It is usually the widow who is left as women tend to outlive their husbands.

We often underestimate the importance of local networks that have been built up over a number of years, and which are taken for granted. We fail to realise that even nodding acquaintances, met when out shopping or walking the dog, can often be crucial in making the day meaningful and may be the only human contact we have with the outside world. They may be even more important when one partner dies and the other is left alone. The few words exchanged, even with comparative strangers, become increasingly significant and can even be the highlight of the day.

It is advisable for those of us who contemplate moving away to a completely new area to get to know the place well before taking such an important step, to see what it is like living there in the cold winter months, as well as in the summer time. We should consider whether there are adequate shops, transport facilities, leisure and entertainment opportunities to suit our particular tastes and to make sure that the environment is one in which it is relatively easy to make new friends, or at least acquaintances.

For all these reasons it is usually better to make such a move fairly soon after reaching retirement age, when it is easier to adapt to what is a very fundamental change, than later on. It is then that the familiarity of our own home, its nooks and crannies, order or clutter, neighbours and local shops and other amenities, become increasingly important as the central focus of our lives. As we get older, it takes longer to become familiar with the immediate surroundings, to be able to put a hand into a cupboard or drawer and know exactly where everything is, or wake up in the middle of the night and remember where we are and find our way to the lavatory.

In a new environment, this process of familiarisation may take as long as one or two years, even for people who are relatively fit and still have fairly accurate memories. Outsiders may interpret the failure to adapt easily as a sign of confusion or it may even be seen as evidence of mental deterioration or senility, in spite of the fact that this type of confusion disappears with time.

Whether we function competently or not depends on the balance between our external world and our own internal world. When young we are able to run or walk confidently over uneven surfaces or along a narrow path. As we get older our internal sense of balance and stability becomes more difficult to maintain. We might easily be toppled by a youngster on a bicycle suddenly appearing from nowhere, or get accidentally jolted by another passer-by. Emotional stability can be similarly put at risk if the move from the family home is made without adequate preparation or is made suddenly. The effect can be similar to that of the youngster on the bicycle or the sudden jolt. Moves are usually easier to cope with if planned well in advance, and if the decisions about the move are our own.

Sheltered housing

An increasing number of older people nowadays wish to consider moving into sheltered housing and this can be a very positive choice. Even so, people should think carefully before moving out of an area they know well. In sheltered accommodation, residents live totally independently in their own flat, or less frequently in a small house or bungalow, but a warden is available. If a resident is taken ill or needs help, someone can be alerted who will be able to make appropriate arrangements or offer assistance.

It is, however, vital to look closely at what is involved, as sheltered accommodation conditions, leases, service charges and other factors can differ. Certain things are fundamental to ascertain in advance, such as the level of support and help available, and whether a warden is on call only in the day time or also at night.

Prospective residents need to know whether they can stay if they become infirm and need more care than a warden usually offers. People who enjoy mixing with others need to pay particular attention to communal facilities, meeting rooms, opportunities for leisure and other activities. It is also useful, if possible, to meet some of the other residents before making the final decision.

Couples need to think about such matters very carefully in advance, but it is particularly important for people on their own to do so, because making new friends is much more difficult than most people realise and their expectations may not be the same as those of the other people living in the sheltered housing complex.

Sharing a family home

There are many loving families where the links between the generations are extremely strong. As people age, these often become the most significant feature of their lives.

Some older people already live with their adult children or they may decide to move in with them. Sharing a home has many advantages. These range from the financial benefits of splitting costs to the close relationships grandparents can have with grandchildren living under the same roof.

The older generation can also be of immense help to hard-working and busy young parents. However, if people are contemplating such a move, the difficulties that could arise also need to be faced beforehand. Each family member should try to spell out exactly what his or her expectations are of the others. For example, young parents may assume that a grandparent will always be available to baby-sit or look after the house, and this may not be at all what the older person had in mind. An elderly parent may, on the other hand, expect to be included in all family meals and social occasions, and this may be similarly unacceptable.

Other questions also need to be addressed. If the grandparents are a close and loving couple who enjoy an intimate and loving relationship, will they have the privacy for this to continue? Are their children able to understand and accept this need or will they or the grandchildren somehow make it impossible, whether intentionally or not? Similarly, will the presence of the older generation restrict privacy and cause difficulties in the relationship between the younger couple, inhibiting their ability to be intimate, to argue, to forgive and to be demonstrably physically close to each other? If the grandparent is alone now or later on, will it be possible for him or her to form new friendships, as might have been the case living away from the family, or will that be considered improper, or even dangerous or ridiculous.

Grandparents also have to remember not to interfere in their children's lives and to allow them to do things their way, even if it seems to the grandparents that they may be making a grave mistake.

As we get older our relationships with those who are dear to us become increasingly important, and it is essential to avoid putting these relationships at risk, however tempting the idea of sharing a home might be. All those involved must make their own decisions, having weighed up the advantages and disadvantages. If it works, the quality of extended family life can be extraordinarily high and give immense pleasure and happiness to everyone concerned.

Sharing with a stranger

There are many reasons for deciding to share a home with a stranger. The financial contribution is obviously important but there are many practical details to work out, such as the use of the bathroom or kitchen, cooking facilities and telephone. Both partners should be quite clear as to the extent of the sharing. For instance, whether they will both use the one living room or what arrangements are made for watching TV or having friends over.

Expectations can also be unrealistic about the quality of the relationship which might develop. It is advisable to think carefully about these factors in advance, discussing the advantages and possible problem areas with adult children or friends and to use a form of written contract, which is available from Citizens' Advice Bureaux.

Sharing with a friend

Some people make a decision to share their home with a friend. As much care needs to be given to this type of arrangement as when couples set up home together when they are younger, because people who like each other and get on well for short periods of time do not necessarily find it easy to share their lives for 24 hours of each day. If they do decide to move in together, it is prudent to retain each person's independent accommodation until both are certain things will work out well. When a decision has been made it is just as essential to work out boundaries for living with a friend as it is with a stranger.

Becoming frail

If we are unfortunate enough to become ill or infirm in our later years and need care, the offer of loving help and support from children, other relatives or friends in their home is often gratefully received and much welcomed. It is, however, advisable to think through questions about the long term implications in advance. It is sometimes difficult to understand how easily a good relationship can deteriorate when a parent who has previously been used to being in charge moves in and is dependent. It may well be that the best or only course of action is to live together but adequate space, privacy and a degree of independent living for all the generations in the household are very important if relationships are to survive rather than disintegrate under the severe strains this involves.

Looking to the future

Loving families and friends would like to feel they were able to care for their parents or elderly relatives or friends according to their wishes. It is difficult for most people to talk about dying and therefore better for the subject to be broached when parents are fit and active. Some people have strong feelings about how they want to be treated if they become terminally ill; whether in hospital, at home or in a hospice, and whether they want all possible measures taken to prolong their lives or not. They may also want to indicate whether they wish to be buried or cremated. Knowing these things have been clarified and arrangements made can only help to ease difficult situations in the future.

Residential care

If we find we cannot manage any longer on our own, another option open to us is to move into a residential home.

This change may be most difficult if it is forced upon us and if we see residential care as the end of the line, the end of privacy and independence and the time when choices will cease. This must not and certainly need not be the case, as residential homes can provide the best form of care for many of us, in settings where our continuing autonomy and independence are fostered.

The old image of residential homes for elderly people has fortunately changed. Most homes today have nothing other than single or double rooms and encourage prospective residents to bring personal possessions and sometimes favourite pieces of furniture to the home with them so that their surroundings have some familiarity about them.

There is a wide variety of homes and it is important to choose one where the atmosphere is congenial, where a wide range of activities is offered and which is convenient for visiting family and friends.

If our emotional lives are to flourish wherever we live, those of us who become frail and dependent to a greater or lesser degree on others, cannot be looked at as isolated individuals. The lives of those who are cared for and those who do the caring are closely interwoven.

10.Caring

'Life is a country that the old have seen and lived in. Those who have to travel through it can only learn the way from them.'

Anon

Many more people are now caring for a frail, chronically sick or disabled elderly loved one than ever before, partly because so many more people survive into extreme old age. Although the vast majority of elderly people remain relatively fit and well, a minority will require continuing help and support. Most stay at home, even when they need constant care. A small proportion end their days in a residential or nursing home or in hospital. Wherever they live people do not necessarily lose all their sexual feelings as they become frail, and they may in fact feel the need for more touching, holding and caressing than ever before.

Caring at Home

Due to medical advances, people do not succumb as easily as they did in the past to infections and acute illnesses, so many more live on when they are physically very frail and in need of increasing levels of care. Therefore carers often find they have taken on a full time job which can last for as many as 10 to 15 years. While this task is generally accepted lovingly and devotedly, it can be totally time-consuming and physically and emotionally draining. The carer may find that without realising it she is providing an increasing amount of care. The initial small amount of help with dressing, cooking or shopping has imperceptibly become full time and a perpetual task, with no time off, seven days a week, often being on call at night as well. It is easy to underestimate the strains the caring role puts on the relationships couples have enjoyed throughout long married lives, as well as on those between parents and their adult caring children. For most carers are 'informal'. That is, they are husbands or sons or, more frequently, wives, daughters, and daughters-in-law, often married with families of their own. Other relatives, close friends or even neighbours sometimes take on the caring without realising what is likely to be involved. They may then find themselves ill-prepared for years of coping with the effects of physical frailty, and even more so with the problems presented by mental infirmity.

Fortunately, lack of preparation does not prevent the majority of informal carers from giving the best possible care to their increasingly dependent loved ones. Often, however, they get locked into an isolated situation where two people become marooned together. Feelings of guilt can easily overwhelm carers simply because they feel the need for some time to themselves.

It can become so difficult for them that they give up all contact with the outside world and themselves become dependent on the person they are caring for. This may be emotionally disastrous when carers eventually have to try to remake their own lives. They then find that they have lost the capacity for making relationships with anybody outside the home.

We are all familiar with sad, isolated people in their sixties and seventies who gave up their own chance of finding a companion when they were younger in order to devote themselves to the care of an elderly relative. With the death of that person very late in life, they find that they have themselves become old and probably have no supportive network around them.

Drawing boundaries

Because care needs increase so insidiously, it is very often difficult for carers to draw boundaries. To withdraw from a task once it has been accepted often leads to hurt feelings on both sides.

Sometimes the caring is shared and a sister, friend or other relative is available to give the carer a few hours to herself and an opportunity to get away and talk to others with fresh ideas. The conversation of someone who is frail and whose horizons have become very narrow can be extremely repetitive and this will add to the carer's feeling of being trapped.

Another problem is that very often the more care frail people receive, the more they demand, and, if they are rarely left alone, they become anxious and demanding if there is no-one in the room with them.

Carers may then find it almost impossible to leave their elderly relative for even a few minutes' shopping. Added to this is the real problem that frail elderly people are more likely to fall if they try to walk by themselves and are more likely to break a bone if they do. They have less strength in their hands than they once had, and may drop things or scald themselves if they try to be independent. The threat of these accidents, major or minor, often increases the carer's feelings of guilt, frustation and anger. With no-one to talk to, it is not surprising that many carers become depressed and irritable with the person they are looking after, even when there is a genuine bond of love and affection between them.

Inevitably taking on a caring role sometimes means that carers give up their jobs to devote all their time to their task. In doing this they may have to live on a reduced income, sometimes putting their pension at risk, and jeopardising their career prospects. This can also have a disastrous effect upon their social life.

Marriages are often put at risk by a daughter being torn between the conflicting needs of an elderly parent and a husband. Sons can also find themselves drawn into a major caring role without realising the strain this can place on their own family.

Things can be equally difficult if disability strikes suddenly. Temporary arrangements are often made which slip into being perm-anent. The intensive care which a loving spouse or child may willingly undertake on a short-term basis, can become an impossible burden over months or years.

Keith and Doris T had been married for 50 years when Doris was taken into hospital with a stroke. She partially recovered but was left with some weakness in one arm and leg, which made it difficult for her to walk by herself although she could manage with help.

She was very unhappy in hospital and as she appeared to be recovering so well, Keith was glad to have her home and made up a bed for her downstairs and they were initially happy to enjoy the physical contact they both had missed while she was in hospital.

They had previously both been quite active and were used to going out on a regular basis but now they stayed at home watching television and eating a lot to pass the time, with the result that they both put on a lot of weight.

There had been talk of getting a wheelchair for Doris but it did not materialise and Keith did not pursue the matter as there were steps leading up to the front door.

Gradually Keith found that he was spending all day caring for Doris and he took to sleeping in a chair downstairs so that he could help her to the lavatory during the night, as she had wet the bed once or twice. Helping her was increasingly difficult due to the fact that she had put on such a lot of weight.

Keith loved Doris dearly but found himself becoming resentful and angry about looking after her. He could see no future for either of them and was shocked to find that from time to time he literally hoped that she would die soon. He became very depressed and went to his doctor, who fortunately realised how serious the situation had become. The doctor managed to arrange respite care for them on a regular basis, combined with day care for Doris when she was not spending time in a residential setting.

Adapting to a caring role can be all the more difficult if it happens suddenly when an elderly relative suffers from a stroke or an illness which makes him or her totally dependent. Particular difficulties can face women who have to look after their father or father-in-law, or men caring for their mother, in having to bath and toilet them, for today's older people are not usually accustomed to seeing even their parent of the same sex naked, and were brought up when taboos about daughters seeing fathers or sons seeing mothers undressed were very strong. These add to the embarrassment and shame that both the carer and the cared-for feel, who may find that the only way of coping with the situation is to be very impersonal and shut off their real emotions. The elderly person may experience this as a coolness which is difficult to understand and may desperately crave for the closer physical contact that the carer is afraid to give.

Turning for help

It helps some carers to join a group and learn from each other's experience. They come to understand that their mixed feelings, their grief, anger and resentment, and at times growing dislike of the person they are caring for, are shared and similarly felt by many others and that the exhaustion, the embarrassment and the impossibility of the full time caring role are at times felt by everyone.

Violet K was a widow of 88. She had struggled fiercely to bring up her four children and had advised and helped them until they reached their present comfortable stage in life. As she became more frail they cared more for her. She appreciated everything that they were doing but was embarassed by being helped with bathing and toiletting and found herself resentful at losing her independence and no longer being in charge of either her life or theirs. She wanted to thank them but found that she was continually finding fault with everything they and their children were trying to do for her. 'Why can't they understand how I feel?' she kept on thinking. They realised that they were 'taking over' more and more but felt that they had to organise her life because they all wanted to share in her care.

Violet became increasingly cantankerous until one day her priest visited her, and realising what was happening, he arranged to see the whole family together with Violet. They were all able to talk about their feelings and work out a way in which Violet was still cared for but felt that she had more responsibility for the things that were happening in her life.

Loss of inhibition

Sometimes people who never spoke about sexuality when they were young or who remained single, even celibate, throughout their lives, lose some of their inhibitions in extreme old age or if they suffer from Alzheimer's disease or a similar mental infirmity. They may become overtly sexually demanding and this can be extremely difficult for carers, especially if looking after a close member of the family, particularly if they are not certain whether to be angry about the unacceptable behaviour, whether to try to change it or to laugh about it. The latter may be very difficult.

Gertie H was a much loved elderly unmarried aunt, who had all her life helped her nieces, nephews and their families whenever there was any problem. She had always been available for emergency baby-sitting or at times of unexpected illnesses and had very often arranged outings, picnics and theatre trips that they had all enjoyed.

Now aged 92, she imagined that every man she saw was making a pass at her. The family called it 'a touch of the Aunty Gerties' and tended to ignore it, but they felt sad that the younger generation were regarding Gertie as 'a batty old lady' while they remembered her as an active, loving person who gave a great deal to all those around her.

For caring relatives, a deeper understanding that sexuality and sexual needs do not necessarily disappear in old age can be a source of strength in enabling them to come to terms with difficult and often apparently unacceptable problem areas. The advice of sympathetic doctors, counsellors and experienced practitioners in nursing, social work and other related professions can be invaluable and should be sought.

Couples in a caring situation often adapt to changed circumstances in remarkably imaginative and satisfying ways. They learn that physical frailty will not in itself remove the need for close physical contact and intimacy and may make it all the more necessary.

When conventional sexual satisfaction is no longer possible, other ways of expressing love and tenderness become more important: the need to be touched, kissed, embraced, to have time to talk and to be near a loved one.

Some couples also manage to relieve sexual tension and meet the needs of a frail partner but if there are problems expert help and advice can be extremely welcome. SPOD and Relate (see *Seeking Help and Advice*) are organisations which can help.

Residential Care

Many carers are 'professionals' – staff working with elderly people in residential or nursing homes or in hospitals. They usually have a particular feeling for old people, otherwise after a short time they would find the job too difficult to cope with.

However, they may, like so many other people, have difficulty in acknowledging that old people have sexual feelings even when they become frail or dependent.

There are sometimes opportunities for people living in a residential setting to form new relationships but it is often difficult due to the physical layout of the building or because they do not have a room of their own. Adapting to life in residential care includes having to live in close proximity to strangers, and sharing a room with one or more other people can make things even harder.

In these circumstances, the way people are treated often predetermines the way that they behave. If they are given no privacy, no chance to make decisions about their own lives, about what time they get up and go to bed, what they eat and whether they go out or not, they are likely to behave like children, becoming dependent, complaining about their 'life' and rebelling against authority. If, on the other hand, they are treated with dignity and encouraged to make as many decisions as possible about daily living, they are more likely to react as adults.

Entering residential care

It is also necessary to remember that many people go into residential care following a crisis, precipitated by a loss, such as the death of a spouse, or by severe illness or disability, all of which can cause severe depression. The move into residential care, coupled with the loss of a much loved home, can easily add to feelings of total despair.

New residents may be totally overwhelmed by what has happened. Therefore it is likely to take at least three to six months for their depression to begin to lift. This may not happen at all without some help, such as counselling, to enable people to examine their losses and try to collect enough strength to begin living positively.

*A*fter Louise W's husband died, she became extremely depressed. Her two daughters lived some distance away and alone in her house she became increasingly miserable and unable to cope. The house got dirtier and Louise didn't bother to feed herself.

One day the milkman noticed that the milk had not been taken in and called the police, who found that Louise had taken an overdose of tablets. She was rushed to hospital and when she recovered, was placed in a residential care home. She hated it there and felt that her daughters did not love her, although they visited her occasionally, and she wished that she was dead.

Jenny, a member of the care staff, felt sorry for Louise and sat with her for long periods, asking her about her past life, her husband, children and grandchildren. Louise gradually spoke more about them and also about her earlier life, when she had been in service in a big house. Jenny was very interested and suggested that she and Louise should write her story and dictate some of it onto a tape recorder, so that her grandchildren would have a record of a *lifestyle that no longer existed. They then began visiting libraries and copying pictures and articles relating to the period and Louise found herself becoming increasingly interested. She was amazed that she also became a focus of considerable interest to the other residents, who wanted to offer help and advice in the project.*

Some elderly people can be helped through counselling or, like Louise, by having an opportunity to talk of their past, but for some the depression is so intense that they need medical treatment. Occasionally they reach the point when their ability to relate to others disappears and without specialist attention they can be wrongly labelled as suffering from senile dementia.

Forming a relationship

The combination of a loss of privacy and the adjustment to communal living necessary when going into residential care can be very difficult for some elderly people. When they also do not have a room to themselves it can be exceptionally hard, particularly if they want to form a personal relationship with another, within which they want to express some physical love and affection.

This may be nothing more than linking arms and occasionally embracing each other but it may extend further, possibly to sharing a bed and making love.

There are some sad stories of elderly couples having to hide their feelings because they could never be sure of being alone. Even holding hands with another person might have to be hidden because of the fear that staff or other residents would disapprove. If there is not even a private room available where couples can meet alone and talk together, there is clearly a tragic lack of understanding about people's needs, at any age.

All adults want and need privacy, and staff should never enter a resident's room until they have knocked and waited for a reply. Even though people are in residential care because they can no longer manage to live without some support, they should never be denied any of the rights other people have, including the dignity of doing as they wish within the privacy of their own rooms, so long as their behaviour does not harm others.

Carers' reactions

Even care staff who care deeply may have difficulty in understanding the full nature of their task. They may see themselves as looking after and caring for older people by washing and dressing them, getting them up and helping them to bed and keeping them fed and warm.

They need training to understand how important it is to help residents live life as fully as possible and make decisions for themselves. They must recognise the abilities old people have and encourage them to use them, rather than concentrating on their disabilities and the things they can't do.

They need to treat each resident with dignity as an individual on an individual basis, trying to find out what he or she wants and matching care to that person's need.

They may have difficulty in understanding how much elderly people need to be touched and held close. Younger staff may easily be embarassed when older people want to kiss and hug them to show their affection, and sometimes fail to realise that they feel as warmly to them as they do to their own families. Occasionally elderly people begin to lose some of their inhibitions and may ask staff to caress or fondle them sexually in the course of bathing or washing. This can be difficult for new staff who will probably not have experienced it before. Like everyone else they will have their own feelings and problems, their own way of life, and their own standards.

There may be problems when residents behave in an openly sexual way in public either by exposing themselves or sometimes by overtly displaying affection, which may not in itself be unseemly, but which may embarrass other residents. Staff have to know how to deal tactfully and sensitively with such situations, explaining that there are some things that are better done in private.

*P*hilip *P was a resident in a home and had upset two members of the care staff who had gone into his room without knocking and had found him masturbating. They were very shocked and went to the head of home to complain and to seek advice. The head of home was able to explain to the care staff that whatever Philip did in the privacy of his own room was up to him.*

It is important for care staff to talk openly together and also with residents about the difficulties and the pleasure that the different manifestations of sexuality can bring to people of all ages and in different states of health, so helping everyone to be more tolerant.

*E*mma *T was an 85 year old resident in a home for elderly people. Whenever a man of any age, from the young doctor to another of the elderly residents approached her, she would stroke him and touch him in a very suggestive manner. The staff considered sending her to a psychiatric hospital. Fortunately an elderly gentleman resident came on the scene and Emma formed a relationship with him. They spent a lot of time together and there were no further problems.*

If the topic has not been raised during training they may not know where to go for help, and be unable to respond appropriately to the resident who may be expressing an unmet need. Just because a need is expressed, it does not necessarily mean that it has to be satisfied. Staff may be very uncertain about what they are expected to do in such circumstances and may even feel guilty that they might have in some way encouraged the resident, if the whole subject seems taboo and not a matter that everyone talks about.

Most people have very little experience of others' sexual behaviour, and some are inclined to assume that everyone else's standards should be the same as theirs. This is particularly likely to happen if they have high moral and religious principles, and they may try to persuade others to behave in the way that they find acceptable. Professional staff who have sexual or marital problems themselves, whether they are aware of them or not, may also at times be judgemental in their attitudes, and their feelings about others may be caused by inadequacies in their own lives rather than a reflection of social attitudes.

*B**ill and Celia C ran a residential home. They had enjoyed no sex life since Bill was 50, when he found that he was no longer able to maintain an erection. He felt sad and aggrieved, but had never talked to his wife about his feelings or asked about hers. They were shocked when they heard that two of the residents were sleeping together and apparently enjoying sexual intercourse. They asked the local authority social worker to have the couple moved. Fortunately the social worker was able to find a training programme for Bill and Celia and this helped them to understand that their unexpressed feelings about their own sex life were influencing their attitude towards people who were very dependent on them and who needed their understanding not their censure.*

Staff also need to accept that some people are homosexual or lesbian. Other residents who will have grown up at a time when homosexuality was illegal and considered sinful may also need help in accepting this.

All staff in residential homes should receive some training in sexuality. This must include giving them an opportunity to discuss their feelings about their own ageing and sexuality and look at the reasons why they might find sexual behaviour in those they care for a problem.

This training may need to take place over a period of time. It can be difficult for some managers to deal with and may be more successful with the help of specialist trainers. They can work closely with members of staff either in groups or individually to help them both to understand their own prejudices and concentrate on the real needs of the people they are looking after, respecting their rights as individuals.

It is particularly important for carers to remember to respect the integrity of those they care for, remembering that ageing is a process almost everyone will experience and that one day they too will know what it is to be old.

None of us should lose our right to experiment, to make good decisions and bad mistakes about all aspects of our social and personal lives as long as we have the capacity to do so. This should not depend on our age or on the value judgements of others, nor be influenced by where we live.

'*Age is opportunity no less*
Than youth itself, though in another dress,
And as the evening twilight fades away
The sky is filled with stars invisible by day.'

Longfellow

Seeking Help and Advice

The following organisations will be able to give advice to people who contact them. If they cannot help directly, they may be able to suggest where specialist services are provided.

Albany Trust
24 Chester Square, London SW1W 9HS
Tel: 01-730 5871

Offers counselling for people with all types of sexual identity and relationship problems. Also runs educational programmes to train and influence individuals and agencies working in personal social services so that they will be better able to help people expressing difficulties with their sexual needs.

Alzheimer's Disease Society
158-160 Balham High Road, London SW12 9BN
Tel: 01-675 6557/8/9

Disseminates knowledge of the illness and the aids and services available. A network of local branches gives support to sufferers and their families. Publishes a newsletter and a number of factsheets and a guide for people caring for someone with dementia.

Amarant Trust
14 Lord North Street, London SW1P 3LD

Promotes better understanding of the menopause and hormone replacement therapy – telephone advice lines are available: the general tape is on 0836400 190 (calls are charged at 25p per minute off-peak and 38p per minute peak).

Arthritis Care
5 Grosvenor Crescent, London SW1X 7ER
Tel: 01-235 0902

Offers information and support on all aspects of coping with arthritis. Local branches.

Association to Aid the Sexual and Personal Relationships of People with a Disability (SPOD)

286 Camden Road, London N7 0BJ
Tel: 01-607 8851/2

SPOD provides an advisory and counselling service for people with disabilities who are in sexual difficulty. SPOD also provides an information service for professional and voluntary workers and education and training on the sexual aspects of disability.

The Association of Sexual and Marital Therapists

P O Box 62, Sheffield S10 3TS

An association concerned about standards of work, training and supervision of therapists. Provides information to the public (SAE please) as to availability of marital and sexual therapy, both NHS and private sector. Serves the UK.

Breast Care and Mastectomy Association

26A Harrison Street, London WC1H 8JG
Tel: 01-837 0908

Provides a non-medical information and support service for women coping with breast surgery.

British Association for Counselling

37a Sheep Street, Rugby CV21 3BX
Tel: 0788 78328/9

Produces a 'counselling and psychotherapy resources directory' listing organisations and individual practitioners providing these services, and indicating fees, specialisations and training. There are some organisations which offer their services free of charge or for a small donation. Guidelines for those seeking counselling are included. Those looking for counselling or psychotherapy offered in their area should either telephone or send an SAE to the above address.

Cancerlink

17 Britannia Street, London WC1X 9JN
Tel: 01-833 2451

Provides information and support about all aspects of cancer. Acts as a resource to cancer support and self-help groups throughout Britain.

Carers' National Association
29 Chilworth Mews, London W2 3RG
Tel: 01-724 7776

Charity founded in 1988 by the merger of the Association of Carers and the National Council for Carers and their Elderly Dependants. It aims to encourage carers to recognise their own needs, develop appropriate support, provide information and advice, and bring their needs to the attention of government and other policy makers.

Catholic Marriage Advisory Council
Clitherow House, 1 Blythe Mews, Blythe Road,
London W14 0NW
Tel: 01-371 1341

Offers a confidential counselling service to anyone needing help in a personal, marital or sexual relationship. The trained Catholic counsellors offer their services voluntarily to any member of the public in need of help.

Chest, Heart and Stroke Association
Tavistock House North, Tavistock Square,
London WC1H 9JE
Tel: 01-387 3012

Offers health education, rehabilitation, welfare and counselling services.

Christian Council on Ageing
The Old Court, Greens Norton, Nr Towcester,
Northants NN12 8BS
Tel: 0327 50481

Works to integrate older people into the life of local churches and communities and improve pastoral care for older people. Runs counselling and pre-retirement courses. A publication list is available.

Colostomy Welfare Group
38-39 Eccleston Square, London SW1V 1PB
Tel: 01-828 5175

Offers information and advice. Will visit patients in their homes where possible.

Cruse – Bereavement Care
Cruse House, 126 Sheen Road, Richmond, Surrey TW9 1UR
Tel: 01-940 4818

Offers counselling, advice and social opportunities to all bereaved people and publishes a range of supportive literature.

Depressives Associated
PO Box 5, Castletown, Portland, Dorset DT5 1BQ

Offers information and encouragement to sufferers and their families. Some self-help groups across the country and national pen-friend scheme.

Divorce Conciliation Advisory Service
38 Ebury Street, London SW1W 0LU
Tel: 01-730 2422

Offers counselling and conciliation services at any stage of divorce proceedings. Free for those on social security.

Family Planning Association
27-35 Mortimer Street, London W1N 7RJ
Tel: 01-636 7866

Gives information and referrals on issues related to sexual and reproductive health. The FPA bookshop 'Healthwise' has many useful books on sex in later life and runs a mail order service.

Gay Men's Disabled Group
c/o Gay's the Word Bookshop, 66 Marchmont Street, London WC1N 1AB

Runs a confidential penfriend service for members and provides a support network for disabled gay men. Maintains a tape library of books on gay topics. Please send SAE.

GEMMA (Lesbians with/without disabilities)
BM Box 5700, London WC1N 3XX

Offers befriending and information services between lesbians with and without disabilities of all ages.

Healthline

PO Box 499, London E2 9PU
Tel: 01-980 4848

Health information by telephone in the form of pre-recorded tape messages. The Service is operated by the Health Information Trust and only costs the price of an ordinary phone call. There are a number of tapes on sexuality – number 184 is on sex and ageing in men and women. You can write to the above address for a copy of the directory leaflet.

Hysterectomy Support Group

11 Henryson Road, Brockley, London SE4 1HL
Tel: 01-690 5987

Self-help groups throughout the country. Publishes newsletter and booklets.

Ileostomy Association of Great Britain and Ireland

Amblehurst House, Black Scotch Lane, Mansfield, Nottinghamshire NG18 4PF

Provides advice and literature; hospital and home visits; and meetings for members through local branches.

Jewish Marriage Council

23 Ravenshurst Avenue, London NW4 4EL
Tel: 01-203 6311

Provides confidential counselling, assisting couples and individuals with relationship problems, whatever their marital status.

Jewish Welfare Board

221 Golders Green Road, London NW11 9DW
Tel: 01-458 3282

Offers a range of local integrated services for older people and their carers; social work with the opportunity to discuss problems, help formulate solutions and receive professional counselling; special daily care units for senile dementia sufferers at hours to suit the carers; and domiciliary care workers providing at home at least part of the care afforded in a residential home.

National Association of Citizens' Advice Bureaux

115-123 Pentonville Road, London N1 9LZ
Tel: 01-833 2181

Founded in 1939 to provide free, impartial and confidential advice and help, through local bureaux, to anyone on any subject. Over 1,000 outlets throughout the UK provide information and advice on areas such as social security benefits, housing, family and personal matters, money and consumer complaints.

National Association of Widows

54-57 Allison Street, Digbeth, Birmingham B5 5TH
Tel: 021-643 8348

Offers information and advice to all widows. Branches throughout the country provide a supportive social role.

National Council for the Divorced and Separated

13 High Street, Little Shelford, Cambridgeshire CB2 5ES

Promotes the interests and welfare of all those whose marriages have ended in divorce or separation. Social activities and counselling centres in several regions and postal advisory service.

National Osteoporosis Society

**PO Box 10, Barton Meade House, Radstock, Bath,
Avon BA3 3YB**
Tel: 0761 32472

Provides information, newsletters and publication for sufferers and sets up local groups.

Parkinson's Disease Society

36 Portland Place, London W1N 3DG
Tel: 01-255 2432

Provides information and literature and helps patients and their relatives with problems in the home. Local branches.

Pre-Retirement Association of Great Britain and Northern Ireland

19 Undine Street, Tooting, London SW17 8PP
Tel: 01-767 3225

Provides and advises on pre-retirement education. Maintains contact with local groups throughout the UK.

Relate (National Marriage Guidance)

Herbert Gray College, Little Church Street, Rugby, Warwickshire CV21 3AP
Tel: 0788 73241

Couples in their 60s, 70s and 80s and beyond can still enjoy good sexual relationships. Difficulties do arise sometimes, and it is sensible to try and sort these out. Relate Marriage Guidance Councils see numerous couples over 60 who find discussing their problems with a counsellor enormously helpful. Couples can refer themselves for confidential counselling to local Relate Marriage Guidance – the number will be in the local telephone book.

Standing Conference of Ethnic Minority Senior Citizens

5-5a Westminster Bridge Road, London SE1 7SW
Tel: 01-928 0095

SCEMSC's activities include counselling and advice for individuals and promoting and developing community care projects.

Tavistock Institute of Marital Studies

Tavistock Centre, 120 Belsize Lane, London NW3 5BA
Tel: 01-435 7111

Provides a professional therapeutic service to those experiencing difficulties with their marriage and sexual problems. Fees are income-related.

Women's Health and Reproductive Rights Information Centre

52-54 Featherstone Street, London EC1Y 8RT
Tel: 01-251 6332/6580

Supplies information on a wide range of women's health topics and works to support a woman's right to sympathetic advice and treatment regardless of race, class, age, sexuality and disability.

Other Publications from Age Concern

All these titles are available from The Marketing Department (LA1), Age Concern England, 60 Pitcairn Road, Mitcham, Surrey CR4 3LL. Cheques or postal orders should be made payable to Age Concern England.

Your Rights 1989/90 by Sally West   *£1.50*

A highly acclaimed annual guide to the State benefits available to older people.

Your Taxes and Savings 1989/90 by Sally West and John Burke   *£2.70*

An invaluable guide to the complexities of the tax system as it affects those over retirement age and of the investment and savings opportunities available to them.

Using Your Home as Capital by Cecil Hinton   *£2.50*

A best selling book for homeowners which gives a detailed explanation of how to capitalise on the value of your home.

Housing Options for Older People by David Bookbinder   *£2.50*

Whether they plan to move or stay put, many older people give some thought to their housing needs in later life. This book sets out to consider all the options open to retired people, both tenants and homeowners, including special housing. Also covered are: financial help with improvement or repairs, home income plans, and how to get special mortgages.

Owning Your Home in Retirement   *£1.50*

Sets out to show how a home can be made more comfortable and easy to manage in retirement. Information on subjects such as repairs and maintenance, heating and insulation, home security and fixtures and adaptations for disabled people are included. Published jointly with the National Housing and Town Planning Council.

At Home in a Home by Pat Young   *£3.95*

There are many questions to ask when elderly people (or their relatives) consider the possibility of residential accommodation: what are the alternatives, what are the pros and cons, and what are the things to look out for when choosing a home? This is a practical guide to help people make the right decisions for themselves.

Loneliness – How to Overcome It by Val Marriott and Terry Timblick   *£3.95*

Contains advice and information on learning to cope with feelings of isolation and includes real-life letters on the subject to Val Marriott – well known 'agony aunt'. The addresses of self-help groups and organisations that can help are also included.

The Magic of Movement by Laura Mitchell   *£3.95*

Another encouraging book by author and TV personality Laura Mitchell for those who are finding everyday activities getting more difficult. Contains gentle exercise to tone up muscles, and ideas to make you feel more independent and to avoid boredom.

Grandparents' Rights by Jill Manthorpe and Celia Atherton   *£3.95*

An invaluable guide to their rights under the law for grandparents separated from their grandchildren through the breakdown of family relationships.

FORTHCOMING TITLES

Famous Ways to Grow Old edited by Philip Bristow   *£8.95*

A collection of letters from a host of internationally distinguished figures outlining their personal attitudes to the onset of old age. Full of amusing and touching anecdotal material.

Life in the Sun by Nancy Tuft   *£6.95*

Written for the increasingly large numbers of older people who choose to move away from Britain, either on a temporary or a permanent basis, this book gives practical advice on all aspects of such an operation, tackling subjects as diverse as what to do with the pets to liability for the 'poll tax'.

We hope you found this book useful. If so,
perhaps you would like to receive further
information about Age Concern or help us do
more for elderly people.

Dear Age Concern
Please send me the details I've ticked below:

other publications   *Age Concern special offers*

☐   ☐

volunteer with a local group   *regular giving*

☐   ☐

covenant   *legacy*

☐   ☐

Meantime, here is a gift of

£ _____   PO/CHEQUE or VISA/ACCESS No _____

NAME (BLOCK CAPITALS) _____

SIGNATURE _____

ADDRESS _____

_____

_____   POSTCODE _____

Please pull out this page and send it to: **Age Concern** (DEPT. LA1)
FREEPOST
Mitcham,
no stamp needed **Surrey CR4 9AS**

About Age Concern

Age Concern England, the publishers of this book as well as a wide range of others, provides training, information and research for use by retired people and those who work with them. It is a registered charity dependent on public support for the continuation of its work.

The three other national Age Concern organisations – Scotland, Wales and Northern Ireland – together with Age Concern England, form a network of over 1,400 independent local UK groups serving the needs of elderly people, assisted by well over 250,000 volunteers. The wide range of services provided includes advice and information, day care, visiting services, voluntary transport schemes, clubs and specialist facilities for physically and mentally frail elderly people.

Age Concern England
Bernard Sunley House
60 Pitcairn Road
Mitcham
Surrey CR4 3LL
Tel: 01-640 5431

Age Concern Scotland
54a Fountainbridge
Edinburgh EH3 9PT
Tel: 031-228 5656

Age Concern Wales
4th Floor
1 Cathedral Road
Cardiff CF1 9SD
Tel: 0222 371821/371566

Age Concern Northern Ireland
6 Lower Crescent
Belfast BT7 1NR
Tel: 0232 245729